BUDDHISM

Volumes in the Religious Traditions of the World Series

Edited by H. Byron Earhart

Religions of Japan *by H. Byron Earhart (published 1984)*
Religions of Africa *by E. Thomas Lawson (published 1984)*
Christianity *by Sandra S. Frankiel (published 1985)*
Religions of China *by Daniel L. Overmyer (published 1986)*
Judaism *by Michael Fishbane (published 1987)*
Buddhism *by Robert C. Lester (published 1987)*
Hinduism *by David M. Knipe*
Islam *by Frederick Denny*
Native Religions of North America *by Åke Hultkrantz*

BUDDHISM

The Path
to Nirvana

ROBERT C. LESTER

1817

Harper & Row, Publishers, San Francisco

New York, Grand Rapids, Philadelphia, St. Louis
London, Singapore, Sydney, Tokyo, Toronto

FIRST EDITION

Designed by Donna Davis

Library of Congress Cataloging in Publication Data

Lester, Robert C.
    Buddhism: the path to Nirvana.

    (Religious traditions of the world)
    Bibliography: p.
    1. Buddhism   I. Title.   II. Series.
BQ4012.L47   1987   294.3   86-43010
ISBN 0-06-065243-8 (pbk.)

        90 91 MPC 10 9 8 7 6 5 4

for Donna

Contents

EDITOR'S FOREWORD

Religious Traditions of the World

One of human history's most fascinating aspects is the richness and variety of its religious traditions—from the earliest times to the present, in every area of the world. The ideal way to learn about all these religions would be to visit the homeland of each—to discuss the scriptures or myths with members of these traditions, explore their shrines and sacred places, view their customs and rituals. Few people have the luxury of leisure and money to take such trips, of course; nor are many prepared to make a systematic study of even those religions that are close at hand. Thus this series of books is a substitute for an around-the-world trip to many different religious traditions: it is an armchair pilgrimage through a number of traditions both distant and different from one another, as well as some situated close to one another in time, space, and religious commitment.

Individual volumes in this series focus on one or more religions, emphasizing the distinctiveness of each tradition while considering it within a comparative context. What links the volumes as a series is a shared concern for religious traditions and a common format for discussing them. Generally, each volume will explore the history of a tradition, interpret it as a unified set of religious beliefs and practices, and give examples of religious careers and typical practices. Individual volumes are self-contained treatments and can be taken up in any sequence. They are introductory, providing interested readers with an overall interpretation of religious traditions without presupposing prior knowledge.

The author of each book combines special knowledge of a religious tradition with considerable experience in teaching and communicating an interpretation of that tradition. This special knowledge includes familiarity with various languages, investigation of religious texts and historical development, and direct contact with the peoples and practices under study. The authors have refined their special knowledge through many years of teaching and writing to frame a general interpretation of the tradition that is responsible to the best-known facts and is readily available to the interested reader.

Let me join with the authors of the series in wishing you an enjoyable and profitable experience in learning about religious traditions of the world.

H. Byron Earhart
Series Editor

Preface

This book is a brief introduction to a large and complex subject. Buddhism is more than twenty-five hundred years old and was defined not only in its native India but also in China, Japan, Tibet, and the several countries of Southeast Asia. The choice of what to include and what to highlight was, to say the least, a painful process. Nonetheless, I believe that the result is a reasonably reliable entre to the origin, development, and major traditions of the Buddhist religion. The reader's understanding of Chinese and Japanese Buddhism can be enhanced by reference to the volumes on the religions of China and the religions of Japan in this series.

In our study of Buddhism it is necessary to become familiar with a certain number of non-English terms. The ancient and authoritative accounts of the life and teachings of the Buddha are written in two languages: Sanskrit and a dialect of Sanskrit known as Pali. Some of the terms useful to our study are the same in both languages; others are slightly different, for example: Tripitaka (Sanskrit)/Tipitaka (Pali), Dharma/Dhamma, Nirvana/Nibbana. To avoid unnecessary confusion, I have used the Sanskrit terminology throughout. In chapter IV, where we are considering specific aspects of the practice of Buddhism in Thailand and Japan, the technical terms are appropriately Thai and Japanese.

The *pin-yin* romanization system is used for spelling out the sound of Chinese characters as approved by the Chinese government. Wade-Giles spelling appears in parentheses for more familiar names, as "Daoism (Taoism)."

Acknowledgments

This book is dedicated to my wife, Donna, my first-level editor. I thank her for putting up with and graciously helping me through the moments of frustration and lack of clarity. I am also grateful to H. Byron Earhart, the general editor of the series and my second-level critic, for his patient and penetrating critique and kindly advice. I commend the several editors at Harper & Row for their careful, well-informed work in finalizing the manuscript for publication.

■

Chronology of Buddhist History

Western Dates	Major Events
563–483 (624–544) B.C.E.*	Life of Siddhartha Gautama, the Buddha
563 (624)	Birth at Lumbini (southern Nepal)
534 (595)	Renunciation
528 (589)	Enlightenment at Bodh Gaya Founding of the Sangha
483 (544)	Death at Kushinara
468 B.C.E.	Death of Vardhamana Mahavira, Founder of Jainism
327–325 B.C.E.	Invasion of northwest India by Alexander the Great
322–185 B.C.E.	Mauryan dynasty; Buddhism spreads throughout northern India
269–232 B.C.E.	Reign of Ashoka Maurya, patron of Buddhism
247B.C.E.	King Tissa of Sri Lanka officially adopts Buddhism
202 B.C.E.–220 C.E.	Han dynasty rules China
200 B.C.E.–200 C.E.	Rise of the Mahayana; Buddhism spreads throughout South India, to Central Asia and to China

*Dates in parentheses are those respected by Theravada Buddhists.

Western Dates	Major Events
140–115 B.C.E.	Reign of Greek king Milinda (Menander)
29 B.C.E.	Portions *of Tripitaka* committed to written form in Sri Lanka
50–200 C.E.	Kushana dynasty rules northwest India and central Asia
78–101	Rule of Kushana king Kanishka, patron of Buddhism
200 C.E.	Nagarjuna, founder of Madhyamika school of Mahayana thought
320–540	Gupta dynasty rules India; rise of Buddhist centers of learning patronized by Gupta kings
300–500	Buddhism introduced to various parts of Southeast Asia; Buddhism rises to prominence in China; Pure Land and Chan (Ch'an) (Zen) Mahayana established c. 500
399	Buddhism introduced to Korea from China
400	Asanga and Vasubandhu, founders of Yogacara school of Mahayana thought; Buddhaghosa produces interpretive texts on Theravada Tripitaka in Sri Lanka
402–411	Fa-xian (Fa-hsien), Chinese Buddhist pilgrim, visits Indian Buddhist centers
538	Buddhism introduced to Japan from Korea
630–644	Xuan-zang (Hsuan-tsang), Chinese Buddhist pilgrim, visits India

Western Dates	Major Events
740–798	King Khri-srong officially establishes Mahayana Buddhism in Tibet
750	Construction of the great Borobudur *stupa* on the island of Java (Indonesia)
760–1142	Pala dynasty rules northeast India, patronizes Buddhist centers of learning
1044–1077	King Anawrahta establishes Theravada Buddhism in Burma
1150	Construction of Angkor monastery and temple in Cambodia
1200	North India comes under Muslim rule; Buddhist centers destroyed; rise of Pure Land and Zen in Japan
1141–1215	Eisai, founder of Rinzai Zen sect, in Japan
1133–1212	Honen, founder of Pure Land (Jodo) sect, in Japan
1173–1262	Shinran, founder of True Pure Land (Jodo Shin) sect, in Japan
1200–1253	Dogen, founder of Soto Zen sect, in Japan
1222–1282	Nichiren, founder of Nichiren sect, in Japan
1275–1317	Rama Khamheng, Thai king, recognizes Theravada Buddhism
1327	King Jayavarman Parameshvara of Cambodia establishes Theravada Buddhism in his kingdom
1360	Fa Ngum establishes Theravada Buddhism in Laos

Western Dates	Major Events
1880	American Henry Steele Olcott spurs Buddhist revival in Sri Lanka
1881	Pali Text Society founded for editing and translation of the Theravada *Tripitaka*
1893	World Parliament of Religions meets in Chicago; speeches by Japanese Zen master and Theravada monk stir American interest in Buddhism
1931	Buddhist Society of America (Zen) founded in New York City
1937	Tsunesaburo Makiguchi founds Nichiren Shoshu Soka Gakkai, in Japan
1944	Buddhist Chruches of America organize, uniting North American temples of Pure Land Buddhism
1950	World Fellowship of Buddhism inaugurated in Sri Lanka
1956	Celebration of 2500 years of Buddhism; B. R. Ambedkar's revival of Buddhism in India
1960	Founding of a chapter of Nichiren Shoshu in California
1968	Tarthang Tulku, Tibetan Buddhist master, begins propagaiton of Buddhism in United States
1970	Chogyam Trungpa Tulku, Tibetan Buddhist master, begins propagation of Buddhism in United States

N

JAPAN

KOREA   Kyoto
         Nara

Kucha (Central Asia)   Beijing (Peking)

AFGHANISTAN   CHINA
GANDHARA
                Shravasti
                NEPAL
PAKISTAN   Lumbini (Nepal)
                Kapilavastu (Nepal)
                Kushinara   TIBET
                Vaishali   Lhasa (Tibet)
        KOSHALA
Mathura   Hanoi
        INDIA   KASHI   MAGADHA
                Sarnath ●Bodh Gaya   VIETNAM
                Banaras   BURMA   ●Pagan
                                                  LAOS
                                            Thaton   THAILAND   ●Angkor
                        ●Amaravati   Bangkok   CAMBODIA
                                                             ●Saigon

                                                                    BORNEO

                ●Anuradhapura (Sri Lanka)
                SRI LANKA

        ┌─────────────────────────────┐
        │   Legend   │   SUMATRA
        │ COUNTRY   │   Palembang
        │ EARLY KINGDOM   │   INDONESIA Borobudur ●JAVA
        │ City   │
        │ ──▶ Spread of Buddhism   │
        └─────────────────────────────┘

■

CHAPTER I

Introduction

Its long history, large number of followers, and global distribution mark Buddhism as one of the major religions of the world. Buddhism arose in India twenty-five hundred years ago, inspired by the life and teachings of Siddhartha Gautama, a wandering monk who came to be known as the **Buddha**,* "the Enlightened One." Today the way of the Buddha has more than five hundred million followers, concentrated in Asia, but also found in significant numbers in Europe and North America. It is the majority tradition of the Asian countries of Sri Lanka, Burma, Thailand, Laos, Cambodia, Vietnam, Tibet, Bhutan, and Japan. By reason of its historical prominence in India, China, Korea, and Indonesia, it has left its mark on cultural values throughout Asia, influencing the behavior of what is today more than two-thirds of the world's population.

I speak of Buddhism as if it were one system of beliefs and practices, everywhere understood and practiced in the same way. This, of course, is no more true of Buddhism than it is of other world religions such as Christianity or Islam. After twenty-five hundred years and adaptation to many different cultural contexts and individual needs, Buddhism encompasses a wide variety of beliefs and practices. There are two major traditions: **Theravada** ("the Way of the Elders") and **Mahayana** ("the Great Vehicle"). The latter is divided into numerous sects, each with a distinctive emphasis. Even within the Theravada tradition there are significant differences of practice from one country to another. The Mahayana is not only divided into sects, but each sect takes a variant form in each of the societies

---

*Terms defined in the Glossary are printed in boldface where they first appear in the text.

in which it is practiced. There is a wide gamut of belief and practice among individuals of the same sect and society. The gap is so wide in some cases that one may wonder how the variants can all belong to Buddhism. Some Buddhists emphasize self-understanding through meditation, others good deeds, and still others the worship of the Buddha. There is no one single Buddhism but many Buddhisms.

Nonetheless, all Buddhisms are Buddhism. There is a common framework for all these variants, a framework that distinguishes Buddhism among the religions and, at the same time, permits and inspires a number of adaptations. Let us begin with an overview of this framework.

Religion is the product of humanity's struggle with finitude, its struggle to overcome suffering and death, to find stability and lasting satisfaction in a world of change. It was the Buddha's perception that instability is inherent in human existence. Reflecting intensely on his body, his feelings and thoughts, and the processes of his mind, he concluded that the human person as well as the natural environment is constantly in flux—from moment to moment arising and decaying—without a permanent substratum. That is to say, in contradiction to popular belief, there is no unchanging soul or God underlying change, only moments passing, each giving rise to the next by its own demise. His reported last words were, appropriately, "To everything that arises, there is cessation; work out your salvation with diligence." He meant, "Be alert, awake; life is passing as quickly as it arises." In this circumstance, according to the Buddha, it is people themselves who cause suffering by trying to hold on to what is incessantly changing—their own life and material possessions. Indeed, humans' belief in a soul and/or a supreme being persisting through time is self-delusion, a feverish attempt to protect themselves in the face of change and death. To be free of suffering, one must renounce all attachments and break through the illusion of permanence by rigorous discipline of body and mind. Self-denial (refusing to lie or steal, to commit violence or engage in sexual misconduct) and meditation will result in enlightenment (**bodhi**)—waking up to life as it really is—and therethrough the cessation of suffering (**nirvana**). Since it is people themselves who, by desire for self-aggrandizement, cause suffering, it is people who must conquer suffering by self-control. The Buddha's prescription for happiness was self-reliance, strict morality, cool rationality, and meditation. He lived the life of a monk, encouraged others to join him in monastic self-denial, and founded a monastic order.

At this point, readers may wonder how Buddhism became a popular religion. The answer lies in the fact that, while the Buddha advocated monasticism, he nonetheless encouraged a lay following and urged the monk to interact with society rather than radically withdraw. He conceived of the layperson as well as the monk as pursuing nirvana, the two at different levels of intensity and in a relationship of mutual dependence. He called his path to nirvana "the Middle Way," a way defined in rejection of both a life of unbridled sensuous enjoyment (hedonism) and a life of extreme self-denial (asceticism). The Path emphasized mental discipline accompanied by physical restraint, not punishment of the body; and it envisaged a progressive discipline beginning with a morality of self-denial practicable in the lay life. Monks were to live in proximity to society as an inspiration, examples of liberating self-discipline, and as teachers. Laypeople were to cultivate self-denial by honoring the monks and giving of their wealth in material support of them.

Furthermore, in time, the Buddha, the order of monks, and even the Buddha's words of teaching became objects of veneration for the laity. The laity came to believe that the self-denial of the Buddha and his disciples created a reservoir of power that could be tapped by prayer and by the recitation and hearing of the Buddha's words, as well as by practicing the teaching and materially supporting the monks. And they believed that this power could effect worldly prosperity as well as progress toward nirvana.

Let us expand on this generalization, leading finally to a compact guideline for understanding Buddhism. The ultimate goal of Buddhism is nirvana—freedom from suffering. Its message begins with the recognition of the fact of suffering in human existence. It characterizes the human person—subject to constant change, pain, and ultimately death—as fundamentally ill-at-ease, full of anxiety, endlessly striving, and never satisfied. According to the Buddha, the cause of suffering is not the natural environment, human society, or the actions of a supernatural force, but humans themselves. More specifically, the cause of suffering is **karma**—the force of a person's thoughts, words, and deeds. Indeed, karma is the cause of life itself. People are self-creating; their physical form is the expression of a mental disposition,

shaped and driven by desire—the desire for life, for pleasure, for power, for possessions, and for freedom. Within certain limits, whatever a
person wills, that is what he or she becomes.

Desire results in thoughts, words, and deeds that have consequences (karma), either for happiness or suffering. Consequences are
basically of two kinds: meritorious (*punya karma*, or "good" karma) or demeritorious (*papa karma*, or "bad" karma). Merit makes
for happiness—good health, long life, high status, wealth, power,
rebirth in a heavenly realm of great pleasure; and, if sufficient, it
results in total freedom from suffering (nirvana). Demerit makes for
unhappiness—poor health, lack of wealth and status, untimely, perhaps violent, death, and rebirth as a subhuman being. The law of
karma necessitates belief in more than one life; indeed, a series of
lives, ended only by the cessation of desire. A person is presently
living as the result of karma from previous lives as well as the karma
so far accumulated in the present life. And accumulated karma at
the end of this life will cause yet another life, perhaps several. Further, future lives may be experienced in other than human forms. In
the Buddha's worldview, there are numerous levels of life-forms,
such as god-forms, animal-forms, and ghostly forms, as well as human forms. Below the earth are realms of punishment; above it are
realms of pleasure (see chart on page 36).

What, then, is the path to merit, to relative happiness, and eventually nirvana? Demerit is the result of action motivated by selfishness, merit the result of action motivated by unselfishness. Selfishness is characterized by lust and hatred and is ultimately rooted in
delusion, in ignorance of the true nature of the self and the world.
Unselfishness shows itself in sexual restraint, nonviolence, non-
possessiveness, and deeds of charity. Moral virtue leads to tranquility
and clarity of mind, qualities conducive to meditation. By meditation, one may attain a state of selflessness or self-negation and know
the self and the world as they really are. This is enlightenment
(*bodhi*), the result of which is nirvana.

The moral perfection and insight necessary for the achievement
of nirvana may take many lives to acquire. Because suffering beings
exist at many different levels of ignorance and selfish attachment,
they require different levels of discipline to alleviate suffering. Ancient Buddhism offered a progressive cure for the selfishness that
causes suffering, a progression from good deeds (**dana**) to morality

(sila) to meditation (**samadhi**). Good deeds, especially deeds of respect and service to holy monks, develop moral character and allow the giver to participate in the merit of the recipient. A morality that precludes violence, lying, stealing, and sexual misconduct cultivates selflessness. Such generosity and morality are appropriate to the lay life—life in family and society. They will eventuate in the ability to live the monastic life, a life of renunciation suitable to full moral purity and meditation. Failing this achievement in one lifetime, the lay person may enjoy rebirth in one of the pleasure realms as a god, and then again return to the human realm in more favorable proximity to the monastic life and nirvana.

Monks withdraw from society to strive for the ultimate perfection and insight. Their greater purity and wisdom permit them to see the suffering of others and give them responsibility to spread Buddha's teachings. They may also exercise the power of their merit and the power of Buddha's teachings on behalf of those who suffer in the world as humans or as wandering hungry ghosts, or those beneath the world, agonizing in hell.

Ancient Buddhism conceived of the lay life and the monastic life as mutually beneficial. The laity shared their goods, giving food, clothing, and housing to monks and thereby permitting the monks a life of strict morality, study, and meditation. Monks shared their merit, their holiness, by receiving offerings from the laity, preaching to them and performing rituals of healing, protection, and blessing on their behalf. Monks were a "field of merit" from which society could harvest blessings.

The path to enlightenment and nirvana begins with faith and proceeds with charity, moral discipline, and meditation. Faith is confidence in the **Three Jewels/Treasures**, the three valued resources for human fulfillment: the *Buddha*, the **Dharma**, and the **Sangha**. This faith is expressed by means of an ancient and still commonly invoked formula, the **Threefold Refuge**:

> I take refuge in the Buddha.
> I take refuge in the Dharma.
> I take refuge in the Sangha.

The *Buddha*, "the Enlightened One," is the historical person Siddhartha Gautama, who lived c. 563–483 B.C.E. He is also a symbol of the realization of truth and the conquest of suffering and an enormous accumulation of power for suffering beings. According to traditional accounts, Gautama left his home and possessions in mid-life to wander as a monk. He turned inward on himself, subduing all desire and clarifying his mind. After six years of rigorous physical and mental discipline, after intense self-analysis and success in destroying all lust, anger, and delusion within himself, he clearly and definitively realized the cause of and cure for human suffering.

The Dharma, "the Doctrine and the Path," is Gautama's teaching. In simple form it is the **Four Noble Truths:**

1. That life is full of suffering;
2. That the cause of suffering is human desire;
3. That the cessation of suffering (nirvana) is attainable;
4. That the eightfold discipline of morality, meditation, and wisdom is the path by which to attain nirvana.

The Dharma is more than Gautama's teaching; it is Eternal Truth, manifested through Gautama; it is powerful by mere invocation; apart from the meaning of the words in which it was spoken.

The Sangha is the community of monks founded by the Buddha and continuing to the present day. In a narrower sense, it is all the saints who through the ages have attained enlightenment. In a wider sense, it is the accumulated holiness and power achieved in a long and continuing tradition of renunciation.

"Taking refuge" in the Buddha, the Dharma, and the Sangha has two levels of meaning. It means following the example of the Buddha by practicing the Dharma as a member of the Sangha. It also means relying on the power of the Buddha, the Dharma, and the Sangha, which is actualized by prayer, ritual incantation, and offerings. The Buddha, Dharma, and Sangha are resources for worldly prosperity—necessary for the achievement of nirvana—as well as for the achievement of nirvana itself. The Buddha is the great teacher and example of one who attains nirvana for those treading the path that he revealed. At the same time, by his meritorious deeds, purity, wisdom, and compassion, he is a reservoir of power for those in need of protection and healing. The Dharma is a pathway to nirvana; it is also the power of the Buddha in words, which, when chanted, control and channel the forces of nature, transfer merit from the living to the dead, and protect against disease and the attack of wild animals. The Sangha is the community of saints and monks striving for nirvana; at the same time, its actual and intended purity and wisdom and its command of the Dharma are power to heal, protect, and bless those who are yet enmired in worldly affairs.

In compact generalization, Buddhism is the pursuit of worldly prosperity, rebirth in heaven, and ultimately nirvana by making and sharing merit (good karma). Nirvana is freedom from rebirth, freedom from suffering. Karma is the force or energy produced by thoughts, words, and deeds. It causes pleasure and pain and rebirth in heaven, on earth, or in hell. Good karma or merit is the result of deeds of charity, moral discipline, meditation, prayer, chanting, and preaching. Making and sharing merit is ultimately for the sake of achieving nirvana—the transcendence of time and space; it is also for healing the sick, channeling the forces of nature, facilitating harmonious family and community relationships, easing the burden of life's transitions, protecting the village, city, and nation, relieving the misery of souls suffering in hell or as wandering ghosts, and attaining a favorable rebirth.

The resources for making and sharing merit are the Three Jewels/Treasures: the Buddha, the Dharma, and the Sangha. They are both the inspiration to the making of merit and the source of merit. The Buddha is "the Enlightened One," the heroic trailblazer of the path to nirvana and an enormous store of merit for suffering beings. The Dharma is the teaching or word of the Buddha that shows the way to nirvana, and it is the expression of the merit of the Buddha, which has power to protect, heal, and give prosperity. The Sangha is the community of monks founded by the Buddha and it is a store of merit for the world.

Our goal is to understand living Buddhism, Buddhism as an existing and ongoing way of life, one of the important value systems of our world. To do so, we shall first have to consider how it came to be and how it developed to become what it is today. Like a person, Buddhism is a product of its history. It has its own "karma," the marks of the accumulated effects of past events. We shall consider this "karma" in Chapter II. Having traced out its development in space and time in Chapter II, having taken it apart, so to speak, in Chapter III we shall then put it back together, looking at it as a unified system of beliefs and practices. Our emphasis will be on the enduring and characteristic features of Buddhism, its essential "logic" as a worldview and as a way of life. With this broad context established, we shall be prepared for Chapter IV in which we shall consider some concrete examples of the living religion.

■

CHAPTER II

The Historical Development of Buddhism

OVERVIEW

Siddhartha Gautama (563–483 B.C.E.) lived in a time of rapid social change resulting in the disintegration of old tribal values. His quest for meaning led to the renunciation of all worldly pursuits and the adoption of the life of a mendicant; as such he was one of many inhabiting the forests of northeast India. He was influenced by the prominent religions of the time, especially **Brahmanism** and **Jainism**, but, in the end, forged his own way. Through rigorous moral discipline and meditation he achieved an insight by which he became known as the Buddha, "the Awakened One." After his awakening, he continued to wander as a monk-teacher, encouraging others to follow the path he had discovered to nirvana, the cessation of suffering. He gave shape to an order of monks (Sangha) supported by lay charity. Highly charismatic, he inspired devotion to his person as well as adherence to his teaching.

The Sangha, charged with a mission to preach the Dharma (the Buddha's teaching) "out of compassion for the world . . . for the welfare of gods and men" and supported by wealthy merchants and rulers, steadily grew, to become a distinctive, highly structured, and powerful institution in Indian society. Lay Buddhism continued to derive its fundamental inspiration from the Sangha, but progressively a cult of devotion to the Buddha was formed that in time significantly altered the whole tradition.

The movement developed harmoniously for the first two hundred years. After 300 B.C.E. distinctive schools of thought began to appear in the Sangha. Increasingly, both lay and monastic Buddhism were influenced by Hinduism and the influx of Greek and Iranian ideas. By the beginning of the Christian era the Sangha was effectively divided into schools adhering to either Great Vehicle (Mahayana) Buddhism or Little Vehicle (**Hinayana**) Buddhism, the latter self-styled as the Way of the Elders (*Theravada*). The elders held to the old ways; the Mahayana set forth a new vision.

After nine hundred years of prosperity, 250 B.C.E.–650 C.E., Buddhism slowly declined to extinction in India. But long before that, Buddhist monks and merchants carried the Way of the Buddha to Sri Lanka and Southeast Asia, through central Asia to China, Korea and Japan, and to Tibet. The Theravada came to dominate in Sri Lanka and on the mainland of Southeast Asia, the Mahayana in China, Korea, Japan, and Tibet. In modern times all of these traditions have come west to Europe and North America, where they thrive, becoming progressively westernized.

The Buddha and His Times

The Record

The chief source of our knowledge of the Buddha and early Buddhism is the authoritative or sacred literature of the Buddhist movement known collectively as **Tripitaka**. Tripitaka, "Three Baskets" or "Three Collections" is made up of *Sutra* ("Discourses")—discourses attributed to the Buddha and embodying his general teachings; *Vinaya* ("Disciplines")—the Buddha's specific pronouncements on the rules of the monastic life; and *Abhidharma*, "The Further or Higher Teachings," formulated by the Buddha's disciples. The oldest portions of this literature, the *Sutra* and *Vinaya*, as we now have them date from about four hundred years after the death of the Buddha. They are based on memories of the Buddha and his teachings, preserved in the monastic community and transmitted orally for two hundred and fifty years (there is evidence that there were written records about 250 B.C.E. but they are not extant). During the oral period, the events of the Buddha's time were reviewed, supplemented, and interpreted again and again as the movement progressed, each addition and interpretation being attributed to the Buddha. This has resulted in a record that reflects two hundred and fifty years of development and in which we cannot clearly distinguish the original teaching from what was added later.

The life story of the Buddha found in this record is an interpretation of the Buddha by his followers over a long period of time and in the light of their belief that he was an extraordinary, wondrous being, an archetype of heroic human existence. We shall consider this archetypal life in chapter III as a key element in Buddhism as a unified system of beliefs and practices. It portrays Gautama as a prince, conceived and born under extraordinary circumstances, married to Yashodhara at the age of sixteen, and productive of a son, Rahula, just prior to renunciation at the age of twenty-nine. If we view the existing record in the light of what critical historians can tell us about the Buddha's period in Indian history, we can conclude only that the Buddha lived during the late sixth and early fifth centuries B.C.E., that he belonged to the Gautama clan of a people known as the Shakyas, that he came to prominence in the kingdoms of Koshala and Magadha as a wandering monk whom many believed to be enlightened, and that he founded a monastic community supported by lay devotees.

Background

Northeast India in the time of the Buddha was divided into small kingdoms and republics according to tribal affiliation. Gautama's tribe, the Shakyas, inhabited the Himalayan foothills along what is today the border between India and Nepal. Gautama wandered the lands of the Koshala, Magadha, Vrijji, and Kashi tribes, spending much of his time in and around their capital cities. The Shakyas were governed by a council of elders, possibly including Gautama's father. They lived on the edge of and paid tribute to the more prosperous kingdoms to the south (Koshala and Magadha) that controlled the fertile lands along the Ganges river and its tributaries.

The economy of the area was based on agriculture. Iron technology had permitted not only more effective weapons of war but also the clearing of the previously forested areas along the Ganges and the development of an increasingly prosperous rice culture. Agricultural prosperity, growing trade, and centralized rule had given rise to large towns and cities—the centers of government, commerce, and guilds of artisans. With the cities and increasing commerce came the mixing of peoples and cultures and the consequent breakdown of old tribal ties and values. One response to this crisis of shifting values was renunciation, withdrawal into the forest for meditation. Gautama was one of many who made this response.

The religious life of the time was dominated by *brahmanas* (priests) and *samanas* (wandering monks). The brahmanas were officiants of a religion of fire-rituals that developed in northwest India beginning c. 1500 B.C.E. among a people known as the Aryans. Brahmanism was an elite religion with worldly goals, based on an ancient revelation called *Veda*. This revelation, effectively known only to the priests, was the instrument for the performance of rituals believed to maintain harmony between humans and a hierarchy of forces (the gods) in the natural world. The offering of food to the gods in fire rituals ensured health, wealth, and good offspring in this life and abode in heaven after death. Brahmanism fostered a highly structured social order, with the priest (*brahmana*) at the top, followed by the warrior/ruler (*kshatriya*), then by the herdsman/farmer (*vaishya*), and at the bottom by the laborer (*sudra*). This hierarchy was believed to be ordained from the beginning of creation and was consistent with the hierarchy of gods and levels of the natural world—sky, upper atmosphere, and earth. As in the natural world the sky directed the activities of the atmosphere and the earth, so in human society the priest ordered the activity of the three lower classes. The high status and power of the priest were guaranteed by his knowledge of Veda and his performance of the rituals by which ordered, prosperous life was maintained.

In renunciation, Gautama joined the *samanas* (literally, "strivers"), homeless wanderers—monks who rejected the settled, worldly life, preferring to live on the fringe of society. They inhabited the forests, living on alms and seeking wisdom through physical renunciation and meditation. By the time of the Buddha a monastic thrust had taken shape within Brahmanism, but it was not well integrated; the *brahmana* and the *samana* essentially represented two different ways of life. The *brahmana* was concerned with ritual purity and social order; the *samana* was concerned with individual moral purity and self-knowledge. The *brahmana* was concerned with worldly prosperity; the *samana* rejected the world in hope of release from the struggle for wealth and power. The *brahmana* was oriented outward, concerned with social structure and rituals by which to worship divine powers; the *samana* turned inward on the self. *Samanas* renounced all function in society and sought a new vision of reality through monastic discipline and meditation; they sought to cut through the illusions and suffering of wealth and power and, as the Buddha put it, "see things as they really are." Having renounced all means of sustenance, the *samanas* relied on householders—rulers, merchants, artisans, and farmers—for food, clothing, medicine, and temporary housing. In exchange they offered their wisdom and healing powers, their blessing to the affairs of their patrons.

Among the *samanas* contemporary with the Buddha was the teacher Vardhamana, known as Mahavira ("Great Hero") or Jina ("The Conqueror"). His disciples were called Jains ("Followers of the Conqueror"). Vardhamana taught the attainment of release of the soul from the material world by extreme asceticism and nonviolence. He went about naked, subjecting himself to discomfort and showing his total rejection of worldly possessions. He taught strict vegetarianism and the rigorous avoidance of the taking of life in any form.

Gautama's Innovation

According to traditional accounts, Gautama studied under two masters of Yoga, a discipline of body and mind whereby one systematically withdraws from all ordinary sensory/mental experience and passes into a succession of trance states. He also tried the extreme asceticism of the Jains, punishing his body by fasting. Finding no lasting satisfaction in these disciplines, he turned to the practice of what he called "mindfulness" (**smriti** or *sati*), a kind of self-analysis in which, rather than trying to subdue or cut off sensory/mental experience, he simply sat, watching his feelings and thoughts as they arose and reflecting on causal patterns.

He realized that his existence was an aggregation of physical and mental states conditioning one another and endlessly arising and passing: "This arising, that arises; this ceasing, that ceases." He realized that his experience of pleasure and pain was conditioned by mental states—states of desire. He felt pleasure when his desire was satisfied and pain when it was not. He knew that a certain amount of pain is inevitable in physical existence, which is constantly subject to change and decay, but he realized that his very physical existence was the result of the force of desire, that desire was merely the surface phenomenon of a complex mental construction—the ego or self-concept. He saw that the mind controls the body, indeed brings it into existence as an instrument of ego satisfaction. The ego patterns or energies that gave rise to present existence were themselves the product of a former existence, the resultant energies of which are called karma. Through the practice of intense mindfulness, aided by certain disciplines of concentration that quiet and purify the mind, Gautama was able to review his karmic stream far into the past. He saw how one life stream gave rise to another, again and again. Having realized this causal pattern, he then saw that since it was desire—the whole ego complex—that caused existence and therefore the physical and mental suffering inherent in existence, subduing and finally extinguishing this ego would result in the cessation of suffering (nirvana). Gautama is portrayed as recounting his enlightenment experience as follows:

> With the mind concentrated, purified, cleansed . . . I directed it to the knowledge of the remembrance of my former existences. I remembered many former existences . . . . There I was of such and such a name, clan, color, livelihood, such pleasure and pain did I suffer, and such was the end of my life. Passing away thence I was born elsewhere . . . . This was the first knowledge that I gained in the first watch of the night. Ignorance was dispelled, knowledge arose . . . . (Then) I directed my mind to the passing away and rebirth of beings. With divine, purified, superhuman vision I saw beings passing away and being reborn, low and high, of good and bad color, in happy or miserable existences according to their karma . . . . This was the second knowledge that I gained in the second watch of the night . . . . (Then) I directed my mind to the knowledge of the destruction of the binding influences [sensual desire, desire for existence, and ignorance.] I duly realized (the truths) "This is suffering . . . . This is the cause of suffering . . . . This is the destruction of suffering . . . . This is the way that leads to the destruction of suffering." As I thus knew and thus perceived, my mind was emancipated . . . . I realized that destroyed is rebirth . . . . There is nought for me beyond this world . . . . Ignorance was dispelled, knowledge arose. Darkness was dispelled, light arose. So is it with him who abides vigilant, strenuous, and resolute.[1]

In common with Brahmanism and Jainism, the Buddha taught that life is conditioned by karma—"the force of deeds." The Law of Karma stipulates that what a person is and does is significantly the result of his or her past deeds, that the circumstances of life—a person's mental and physical capacities, the social and economic situation into which a person is born, and the ongoing events of life—are not accidental or caused by some outside force but are the fruit of a person's own past lives as well as the present one. Karma implicates all living beings—animals and insects as well as human beings—in a series of births and deaths (**samsara**), the present life being the fruit of past lives and, in turn, contributing to the shape of future lives. The Brahmanas and Jains called this process "transmigration," believing that living beings possess an eternal, unchanging soul (*atman*) that "crosses over" from one body to the next at death. The Buddha rejected the idea that any such eternal, unconditioned entity—soul *or* God—exists. His self-analysis revealed that everything that makes up a living being, as well as everything that makes up the natural world, is constantly changing, arising and decaying moment by moment. Inasmuch as one complex of fleeting elements decays, at what is commonly called "death," and gives rise to an initial complex of elements that shapes another body, we can speak of "rebirth"—but not transmigration; nothing unchanging carries over. This same rebirth is occurring every moment in what we call life.

Indeed, according to the Buddha, it is the belief in the fact of or possibility of permanent soul/selfhood (*atman*) that causes all human suffering and dissatisfaction. The core of the Buddha's discovery in becoming enlightened was the realization that life is a mass of suffering and this suffering is caused by desire—desire for life, for pleasure, for status, for possessions—which is rooted in belief in self. His prescription for the good life—freedom from suffering—was moral and mental discipline leading to insight into the true nature of life and therewith the extinction of desire. The desireless state, the goal of his teaching, he called nirvana, "extinction" (of the flame of desire).

Brahmanism, Jainism, and Buddhism respected the same moral principles (nonviolence, sexual restraint, and prohibitions against lying, stealing and alcoholic drink), but in Brahmanism morality was secondary to ritual purity, that is, ritual correctness based on knowledge of Veda. Jainism and Buddhism emphasized knowledge of the self through meditation. They parted company on the degree of rigor in moral discipline.

The Buddha offered his insight as "the Middle Way," defined by the rejection of worldliness *and* asceticism, Brahmanism and Jainism. He rejected the *brahmana*'s claim to superiority by reason of his knowledge of Veda and performance of the fire rituals. He rejected the *brahmana*'s concern with worldly riches. Instead he preached the simple life that renounced attachment to worldly goods and was concerned for moral character and self-knowledge through discipline. He did not reject the gods of Brahmanism but subordinated their power to the one who has conquered all desire. At the same time, he rejected the extreme asceticism of the Jains, which he considered "painful, ignoble, and useless." For the Buddha, the goal of self-discipline was not the punishment and death of the body, but the serenity of mind and body through the extinction of desire.

The Formative Period: 500–250 B.C.E.

Monks and Laity

According to the record, the Buddha wandered for forty-five years after his enlightenment, teaching and gathering both lay and monastic disciples. He is portrayed as teaching the laity the merits (good karma) of giving alms to those who have taken up the homeless life and of keeping the five moral precepts—abstention from taking human life, lying, stealing, illicit sexual activity, and alcoholic drink. He taught charity and morality as the means to harmony and prosperity in this life and a favorable rebirth in the next. To those he perceived ready, he taught "the higher dharma," the truths of suffering, its cause, its cure, and the monastic path leading to nirvana.

In general, *samanas* avoided contact with society as much as possible. The Buddha instructed his monks to "wander alone, like a rhinoceros," to have no refuge but the Dharma. But this did not mean that they were to avoid all contact with society. The Buddha rejected the life of extreme asceticism—total withdrawal and the practice of physically punishing disciplines; he instructed the monks to teach the Dharma, "for the welfare of the many." Most important of all, he encouraged both lay and monastic disciples and taught them a life of mutually beneficial dependence. We might say that the Buddha made a virtue of necessity. Monks, whose discipline prohibited them from working to provide the necessities of life, would benefit by the laity's gifts of food, clothing, medicine, and temporary housing. But the monks were not to be seen as an unproductive drain on society. The laity would benefit by the teaching of the monks and by the good karma they would accumulate as the result of giving. This karma would result in a more favorable rebirth and eventually a life in which the layperson would be ready for the monastic pursuit of nirvana.

They pay you great service, O monks, the Brahmins and the householders who give you clothing, alms, seats, couches, and medicines. You also pay them great service when you teach them the Good Doctrine and the pure life. Thus it is through your mutual help that the religious life, which causes the crossing over beyond rebirth and puts an end to suffering, can be practiced. Each relying on the other, householders and homeless cause the Good Doctrine to prosper. The latter are protected from need, since they receive clothing and the rest; the former, having practiced the Doctrine in this world, the Path which leads to good forms of rebirth, delight in the world of the gods possessed of the blisses.[2]

In five ways should the clansman minister to recluses: by affection in act and speech and mind; by keeping open house to them, by supplying their temporal needs. Thus ministered to recluses . . . show their love for the clansman in six ways: they restrain him from evil, they exhort him to good, they love him with kindly thoughts; they teach him what he had not heard, they correct and purify what he has heard, they reveal to him the way to heaven.[3]

Monks, by their purity and wisdom, were a reservoir of goodness, a "field of merit" for society.

The Lord's order of disciples [Sangha] is of good conduct . . . worthy of alms, worthy of hospitality, worthy of offerings, worthy of reverence, it is a matchless field of merit for the world.[4]

The laity were eager to provide for the monks. They saw them not only as a source of wisdom and an example of purity of life, but also as possessed of special powers by reason of their wisdom and purity. They believed that the very presence of a monk would subdue forces of misfortune and disease and create an air of prosperity. The Buddha is portrayed as dispelling malicious spirits who had brought disease to the city of Vaishali and as subduing wild animals. It is said that he gave his disciples verses called **paritta** ("protection"), by the pronouncement of which they could avert danger and create an auspicious environment.

Early Disciples

A wide variety of persons, women and men, responded to the Buddha's message. The first sixty he received into the monastic life were five *samanas* and fifty-five merchants "of prominent families." These sixty are said to have quickly attained the status of **arhat**, "holy one," in whom all desire was extinguished and for whom there would be no further birth. The Buddha then sent them forth to "wander, for the gain of the many, for the welfare of the many, out of compassion for the world," to preach the Dharma and "proclaim a consummate, perfect, and pure life of holiness."[5] Many *brahmanas* joined the Sangha, among them Sariputra and Maudgalyayana, who became the Buddha's chief disciples. Sariputra was known for his great wisdom and Maudgalyayana for his supernormal powers.

After an initial ministry in Magadha, the Buddha returned home to Kapilavastu, the chief city of the Shakyas, and there received his son, Rahula, two cousins, Ananda and Devadatta, and one of their attendants, Upali, a barber, into the monastic life. Ananda became the Buddha's companion and valet in later life. Devadatta, brother-in-law as well as cousin to Gautama, endeavored to rival the Buddha for leadership of the monastic community but was not successful. He is portrayed as bearing resentment toward the Buddha in spite of his monastic vows for the Buddha's having left his wife (Devadatta's sister) in renunciation. Upali, the barber, was one of several persons of the lower social classes who joined the Sangha; Upali and Ananda were remembered as the two who rehearsed the entire teaching of the Buddha before a great assembly of monks just after the master's death.

Reportedly, with strong reservations the Buddha agreed to allow women to undertake the monastic life. Mahaprajapati, the second wife of the Buddha's father (his first wife, the Buddha's mother, died a few days after giving birth to Gautama), became the first nun. The record of early monastic life pays very little attention to the nuns but it does show that a significant number of women were attracted to the order, many of them widows without children.

The prominent lay disciples of the Buddha came from the merchant and ruling classes—the father, mother, and wife of Yasa, a wealthy merchant who himself became a monk; King Bimbasara of Magadha; the Buddha's father; and Ambapali, a wealthy courtesan. This is only to identify those who, it is said, made a formal commitment to the way of the Buddha. The laity that played a crucial role in the early development of Buddhism included householders in general. Even those who had no particular knowledge of or commitment to the teachings of the Buddha were drawn to respect and support these new *samanas* in hope of being blessed by such contact.

Those who entered upon the homeless life committed themselves to a highly demanding morality and daily regimen. They were not to take life in any form; they were not to lie, steal, engage in sexual activity, drink alcoholic beverages, participate in any form of entertainment, use comfortable seats or beds, handle money, or eat more than one meal per day. They were permitted a minimum of possessions: a food bowl, a razor, a water strainer, a needle, and a staff. At first, they followed a way of life common to all *samanas*: wandering, dwelling and meditating in the forest, wearing castoff rags, begging for their food, and using only cow's urine for medicine. In time, the Buddha permitted those who wished to dwell near a village for ease of access to food, to accept gifts of robes from the laity, to accept invitations to eat in the homes of the laity, and to use a variety of medicines depending upon their need. Some, who came to be called "forest dwellers," continued to keep the old rule; the majority became "village dwellers." This distinction persisted and exists today in Theravada Buddhism.

Monks wandered, then entered a village for food, rested, meditated, and received and instructed lay visitors; they left the village to sleep outside of it at night, then moved on the next day. This was their pattern except during the rainy season, a period of approximately four months from mid-June to mid-October, when it was difficult to move about and customary for *samanas* to take shelter. Some of the monks constructed temporary housing in the forest and kept largely to themselves in study and meditation. Most followed the Buddha's example and sought shelter in close proximity to a populated area where they could conveniently beg for food. It is recorded that, among others, the king of Magadha, the wealthy merchant Ananthapindika, and the courtesan Ambapali each donated pleasant groves for the use of the Buddha and his monks. During the rains, the monks gathered in such places, especially where they might be with the Buddha. This kind of **rain-retreat** fostered the development of a communal life among the monks and encouraged more than the usual contact between monks and laity.

After Buddha

In the course of time, with the approval of the Buddha, the monks fashioned an elaborate code of behavior and an administrative structure for communal living. They also developed a number of community rituals, in some of which the laity were invited to participate. After the Buddha's death, the monks intensified their communal life in mutual support and in preserving the teaching and way of life. In the absence of the charismatic leader, solidarity gave authority to the teaching and tended to maintain the purity of the lifestyle; regularized ceremony heightened the sense of authenticity and power of the monastic way. The laity strongly encouraged such developments by providing more and better amenities for the monks' sojourn during the rains. Desirous of the opportunities for merit making afforded by the continuous presence of monks, the laity were just as concerned about the welfare and purity of the monks as the monks were themselves. The monks tended to return to the same places year after year. The laity constructed more and more permanent and elaborate dwellings and ceremonial halls, until what had begun as informal, temporary gatherings had become more or less settled monastic communities, each with a defined boundary and a particular membership.

The first two hundred years of the Sangha was a process of gradually settling and formalizing the monastic life. After the death of the Buddha, there was no centralized authority. The Buddha did not appoint a successor; rather, he instructed his followers to be governed by the teaching (Dharma). Nevertheless, under the guidance of senior monks, uniform rules, regulations, and rituals evolved and were generally respected. According to the *Vinaya*, immediately following the death of the Buddha, five hundred monks gathered in rain-retreat jointly confirmed the teaching as recited by Ananda and Upali. A similar council one hundred years later again reaffirmed the authoritative teaching. Monastic rule and ritual as practiced today were fully formulated by 250 B.C.E. Each community was autonomous and self-governing by consensus of the gathered body under the guidance of elder monks.

So long, O mendicants, as the brethren meet together in full and frequent assemblies—so long as they meet together in concord, and rise in concord, and carry out in concord the duties of the order—so long as the brethren shall establish nothing that has not been already prescribed, and abrogate nothing that has been already established, and act in accordance with the rules of the order as now laid down—so long as the brethren honor and esteem and revere and support the elders of experience and long standing, the fathers and leaders of the order, and hold it a point of duty to hearken to their words . . . so long may the brethren be expected, not to decline, but to prosper.[6]

The elders gathered the Buddha's remarks on what was prohibited in the monastic life into a code of discipline called the **Pratimoksha**, or "Bond of Unity." This code includes 227 prohibitions in order of seriousness of offense and beginning with what the Buddha called "The Four Things Not to Be Done." A monk

1) Ought to abstain from all sexual intercourse even with an animal; 2) ought to abstain from taking what is not given to him, and from theft, even of a blade of grass; 3) ought not intentionally to destroy the life of any being down to a worm or ant; 4) ought not to attribute to himself any superhuman condition.[7]

Offense against these four prohibitions resulted in expulsion from the order. Offense against the other prohibitions entailed one degree or another of penance and forfeiture of privileges, to be determined by the gathered community, or simply confession of the offense to another monk.

The elders set forth a separate *Pratimoksha* code for nuns, containing more than double the number of rules for monks. It is said that when the Buddha permitted women to join the Sangha, he did so only with the stipulation that nuns be strictly subordinate to monks. He specified, for instance, that women, regardless of age, spend a minimum of two years probation as novices before full ordination; that they be ordained by an assembly of monks as well as by an assembly of nuns; that nuns reside only in an area in which there are monks; that they honor all monks as their seniors; and that they accept criticism from monks without the privilege of giving it. In placing such special restrictions on women, the Buddha reportedly had a twofold concern: that women not be encouraged to renounce their household responsibilities in order to join the Sangha; and that, should they do so, their presence must not corrupt the order.

Inspired by a Brahmanical practice of purificatory rites on the day before the new-moon and full-moon fire sacrifices, the Buddhist elders prescribed that the *Pratimoksha* code should be jointly recited in each monastery on these days each month. This "Observance" (*uposatha*) as it was called, came to be a time when monks would confess any infraction to a fellow monk before engaging in the communal recitation. Lay devotees were invited to spend this day at the monastery, observing a discipline of fasting and keeping the basic precepts of the monastic life. Following the recitation, the laity were permitted to sit in the presence of the monks to hear a sermon by one of the elders. Observance days became a vital link between monk and laity, in importance second only to their daily contact in the giving and receiving of food.

Ordination

The Buddha reportedly received those desirous of undertaking the monastic life with a simple invitation:

> Come, O monk. Well taught is the Dharma; lead a holy life for the sake of the complete extinction of suffering.[8]

After his death, reception into the order became a formal act of ordination, increasing in complexity as the order grew in size and became more and more formally constituted. Concerned that the new initiates, especially young men in their teens, might not be prepared for the full rigor of monastic life, the elders instituted a probationary or novitiate ordination (*pravrajya*). The novice had to be at least fifteen years of age and was assigned a preceptor, or "big brother," and a teacher, who supervised his conduct and learning throughout the probationary period. The ordination procedure was as follows.

> Let him first have his hair and beard cut off; let him put on yellow robes, adjust his upper robe so as to cover one shoulder, salute the feet of the monks with his head, and sit down squatting; then let him raise his joined hands and tell him to say: "I take my refuge in the Buddha, I take my refuge in the Dharma, I take my refuge in the Sangha."[9]

Following the recitation of the Threefold Refuge three times, he was instructed in the **Ten Precepts**:
1) not to take life;
2) not to lie;
3) not to steal;
4) not to engage in sexual activity;
5) not to drink alcohol;
6) not to take food from noon to the next morning;
7) not to adorn their bodies with anything other than the three robes;
8) not to participate in or be spectator to public entertainments;
9) not to use high or comfortable beds;
10) not to use money.

It was determined that the candidate for full or higher ordination (*upasampada*) had to be at least twenty years of age, free of serious illness, and free of any social obligation (e.g., debt or obligation to military service). He had to have the permission of his parents or wife, as the case may be. His ordination required the presence of at least ten monks and committed him to the full *Pratimoksha* rule.

Ordination was a special occasion for the laity, especially the parents and relatives of the candidate, to receive merit. They attended the ritual, bearing small gifts for the monks. Ordinations most frequently occurred just prior to the rain-retreat, thus affording the new initiate a time of intensive training under close supervision. It was likely also that, at an early time, the laity believed that the merit-force created by the act of renunciation by virile young men would stimulate rainfall for the crops. No formality was prescribed for entrance into rain-retreat, but the retreat was to be concluded with a ritual "Invitation" (*pravarana*) by each monk to the gathered body to inform him of infractions he may have committed during retreat.

As noted above, the Buddha permitted the monks to receive robes as a gift from the laity. The opportune time for this giving was at the end of the rain-retreat when the monks prepared to wander. Thus, the elders prescribed a ritual called Kathina (*kathina* means "rough cloth") at which the laity formally presented cloth and the monks prepared and distributed new robes. Kathina became another special link between monk and laity.

The monk was permitted ten items: three robes—an outer garment, undergarment, and a cloak—a food bowl, a belt, a razor, a needle, a strainer, a staff, and a toothpick. The daily regimen of the monk, whether residing in a monastery or wandering, became quite standardized. He was to rise early, well before dawn, cleanse himself, and sit quietly in meditation until the time (dawn) to enter the village for food. In the village, he was to walk without speaking, with his gaze downward, receiving food in his bowl at random, wherever it was offered. He was permitted to receive certain kinds of meat, as long as he was not aware that it had been specially prepared for him. Returning to the monastery or his place outside the village, he was to eat in silence, taking the food from the bowl in whatever order it had been placed there and reflecting to himself on food as medicine for a wound. According to the precepts he had to finish eating before noon. Thereafter, if a novice, he would receive counsel from his preceptor or instruction from his teacher; if a senior monk, he would engage in instructing others. Midafternoon was a time for quiet sitting and/or napping, after which he received guests. In the evening he returned again to study or instruction before retiring for the night.

The early monastic communities were self-governing units. Each had a specified geographical boundary and a certified membership, in accordance with the commonly accepted monastic code. The code was generally respected by secular authority. Adherence to the discipline was policed by fellow monks (peer pressure), laity, and, when necessary, by a formally constituted meeting of the entire monastic community. Important issues were settled by consensus. Seniority,

determined by the number of years since ordination, was respected
and seniors consulted, but senior monks had no formal authority.
The gathered community appointed a senior monk as chief adminis-
trator and he, in turn, appointed other functionaries—overseers of
buildings, robe and room distribution, and so on, as the community
had need.

Early Appeal

In the early centuries of the movement, Buddhism had greater potential for mass support than either Brahmanism or Jainism. In
Brahmanism the concern for ritual purity, expressed in a well-de-
fined class structure, set the priests apart from the people. The sacred knowledge of Brahmanism, the Veda, was transmitted in an
elite language and was known only to the priests. The Buddha's
words were carried in the vernacular languages and freely shared.
Class status was of no concern to the Buddha; moral character rather
than ritual purity was the basis for status. Jainism, although it developed a strong lay following, separated the monk from the laity
more sharply than Buddhism by its extreme asceticism. This extreme posture was confrontational rather than conciliatory. The
Buddha's Middle Way rejected both asceticism and worldliness and
strongly encouraged lay participation and the close proximity of
monks and laity. The monastic communities were visible and available to the people. His teachings were accommodating rather than
confrontational; they subordinated and reinterpreted most existing
religious beliefs and practices rather than pushing them aside.

The monastic life appealed to a significant number of persons,
both female and male, especially those in need of security. As members of the Sangha, they enjoyed not only the necessities of life but
enormous prestige. To warrant this status they had to maintain a
somewhat demanding way of life, but the discipline was not oner-
ous once the initial adjustment had been made.

The settled, well-ordered Sangha pursuing a nonviolent life-style
also appealed to local rulers and the general populace. Not only was
the Sangha a peaceful influence, but also, the laity desired to benefit
from the merit of the monks. The more they invested in the monks
and monasteries, the greater the merit for them. With the provision
of permanent, well-furnished dwelling places, the monks wandered

less. In any event, there were always some monks present, appointed to maintain the monastery.

The laity had opportunity for daily contact with the monks in providing them with food. The monks were readily available and anyone could give alms. This became a ritualized act of great merit. The laity had opportunity to consult with the monks at the monastery and on Observance days to receive instruction and blessing at their feet. Participation in an ordination by provision of amenities to the ordinand and the order of monks or simply by presence at the ceremony came to be seen as an opportunity for great merit, especially for the parents and friends of the new monk or nun.

The early lay practice of Buddhism was dependent upon the monastic community, with one important exception. The laity initiated the practice of venerating the remains of the Buddha and his most renowned disciples. According to the *Tripitaka*, the Buddha himself authorized the burial of his cremation remains in a mound at a crossroads, where travelers might honor his memory and thereby be assured of rebirth in heaven.

> And as they treat the remains of a king of kings, so, Ananda, should they treat the remains of the **Tathagata** ["the One Thus-come" or "Thus-gone"]. At the four cross roads a *thupa* should be erected to the **Tathagata**. And whosoever shall there place garlands or perfumes or paint, or make salutation there, or become in its presence calm in heart—that shall long be to them for a profit and a joy . . . . At the thought, Ananda, "This is the *thupa* of that Blessed One, of that Arahat-Buddha," the hearts of many shall be made calm and happy; and since they there had calmed and satisfied their hearts they will be reborn after death, when the body has dissolved, in the happy realms of heaven.[10]

A *thupa* (Sanskrit, **stupa**) is a mound of earth. The practice of building a mound over the remains of great persons as a place of remembrance and worship is very old in India, predating the Buddha. The Buddha instructed Ananda that the cremation and enshrinement were not to be performed by the monks but were to be left to the laity. Reportedly, the bones and ashes of the Buddha were divided into eight portions and distributed to eight parties of the laity who enshrined them in various locations. Whether or not this actually occurred immediately after the Buddha's death, such memorialization of the Buddha is very old and quite understandable. From all accounts, the Buddha was a highly charismatic personage, an imposing and compassionate presence. Furthermore, he himself urged the laity to respect and benefit from the power of holy monks. The development of *stupa* worship was based on the belief that the great merit and compassion of the Buddha continued to radiate from his remains. In effect, the *stupa* marked the continuing presence of the Buddha.

In time, the practice of erecting *stupas* became a hallmark of Buddhism. With the development of brick and plaster construction techniques, multileveled, relatively permanent, and sometimes quite large structures replaced the simple mound of earth. The most powerful *stupas* were those erected at places believed to have been frequented by the Buddha, and worship at *stupas* came to be closely associated with the practice of pilgrimage. Pilgrimage to the birthplace, the place of enlightenment, the place of the first sermon, and the place of the death of the Buddha is authorized in the same discourse in which the Buddha speaks of the *stupa*. As with *stupa* worship, great merit results from pilgrimage:

> And they, Ananda, who shall die while they, with believing heart, are journeying on such pilgrimage, shall be reborn after death, when the body shall dissolve, in the happy realms of heaven.[11]

Early Buddhism assimilated the gods and spirits of Brahmanism and popular folklore, interpreting their nature and existence in terms of karma—merit and demerit. They are conceived as part of a hierarchy of life forms running a gamut from existence in extreme pain to existence in great pleasure as the result of good and bad deeds.

The Sixfold Hierarchy of Beings

I. The Realms of the Gods—twenty-two levels, above the earth, e.g.:

Sublime Gods
Richly Rewarded Gods
Radiant Gods
Great Brahmas   increasing
Satisfied Gods   pleasure
The Thirty-three Gods (of Brahmanism)

II. The Realm of Humans—mixed pleasure and pain

III. The Realm of Demons, in the atmosphere, near the earth   increasing
IV. The Realm of Hungry Ghosts, on the earth   pain
  V. The Realm of Animals
VI. The Realm of Hell-dwellers, below the earth

Human existence is the middle tier of this hierarchy, a realm of mixed pleasure and pain. Merit and demerit (good and bad karma) are created only in the human realm. Its effects are experienced, appropriately, in one or another of the six realms. Gods, demons, ghosts, animals, and hell-dwellers do not produce karma; they only live out the effects of karma produced in the human realm. Demerit earned as a human leads to rebirth as a demon, a hungry ghost, an animal, or an inhabitant of hell; merit leads to rebirth as a god or, again, as a human being. Those who grasp for power are condemned by such karma to a life as a powerful demon. Those who are unduly attached to family, money, and possessions are reborn as hungry ghosts—invisible beings that roam and haunt the earth suffering insatiable hunger. Preoccupation with food and sex leads to life as an animal; and a life dominated by violence, hatred, and anger leads to the most extreme punishment—life beneath the earth, in hell. On the other hand, generosity, morality, and meditation result in rebirth in the happy realms as a god or return again to the human realm in a position more favorable for the achievement of nirvana. These nonhuman forms of existence may last millions of years; still, like human existence, they are temporary. When a being's store of merit is exhausted as a god, he or she returns again to the human realm with another opportunity for merit and nirvana; or, perhaps, if there is sufficient demerit remaining from the former human existence, he or she falls to a realm of punishment to work out this demerit. Likewise, when demerit is exhausted, a hungry ghost, for instance, may revert to human form or rise to a realm of pleasure.

The activities of the various nonhuman beings may impinge upon life in the human realm for good or ill. The actions of malicious spirits may be curbed or warded off by the power of the monks and recitation of words of the Buddha; the power of the Buddha, the Dharma, and the Sangha is far greater than that of gods or demons. Certain of the gods have power over certain forces of nature or malevolent spirits and may be invoked for protection or blessing on special occasions. Furthermore, just as the monk can share merit with the laity, so human beings can share merit with those languishing in one of the realms of punishment, some of whom may, indeed, be their relatives.

From Ashoka to the Guptas: 250 B.C.E.–300 C.E.

The spread and prosperity of Buddhism in India was greatly assisted by the patronage of kings. Magadha was the heartland of Buddhism. The Magadhan kings Bimbasara and Ajatasatru, contemporaries of the Buddha, patronized the Sangha. Their successors gradually rose to power over all India. In 327 B.C.E. the Greeks conquered northwest India under Alexander the Great. Alexander crossed the Indus River and then gave up the campaign and re-

Pillar-capital of King Ashoka, at Sarnath, where the Buddha preached his first sermon. The Buddha's preaching of the Dharma, symbolized by the wheel, came to be referred to as "the lion's roar." The animals accompanying the dharma wheel around the midsection of the capital—an elephant, a bull, a horse and a lion— are taken to symbolize the conception, birth, renunciation and first sermon of the Buddha.

turned to Macedonia, leaving governors in charge of the conquered area. His brief entrance and exit created a power vacuum such that, shortly thereafter, under the leadership of Chandragupta Maurya (reigning 322–297 B.C.E.), the Magadhans extended their rule all across northern India. Chandragupta's successors conquered to the south. Magadhan pacification and unification of the subcontinent encouraged the spread of Buddhism.

Ashoka Maurya (reigning 260–232 B.C.E.), the third emperor of the dynasty, left a record of his activities and ideals in edicts written on rocks and pillars. The edicts show that, in remorse after a conquest in which several hundred thousand people were killed, Ashoka declared that henceforth he would rule by Dharma. His *dharma* emphasized:

> . . . abstention from killing animals and from cruelty to living beings, kindliness in human and family relations, respect for brahmanas and samanas and obedience to mother, father and elders . . .[12]

The declared reward for living in accord with this *dharma* is peace and prosperity in this world and abode in heaven after death. Ashoka declared himself to be a lay follower of Buddhism; his edicts note that he made pilgrimages to the Buddha's birthplace at Lumbini, the place of the great enlightenment near Gaya, and the place of the first sermon at Sarnath. Edicts at Sanchi and Sarnath show that he exhorted monks to study the Buddha's teaching and adhere to it without schism in their ranks. Although himself a follower of Buddhism, his official policy recognized and supported all religions.

> My officers charged with the spread of Dharma are occupied with various kinds of services beneficial to ascetics and householders, and they are empowered to concern themselves with all sects. I have ordered some of them to look after the affairs of the Sangha, some to take care of the Brahmin . . . some to work among the Nirgranthas [Jains] . . . [13]

According to a chronicle compiled in Sri Lanka by Buddhist monks in the fifth century, Ashoka's rule was the archetype of Buddhist kingship. The chronicles say that he constructed eighty-four thousand monasteries and *stupas*, and that to purify and preserve the Sangha, he convened a great council of monks at his capital, Pataliputra (modern-day Patna). The council dismissed some sixty thousand monks who had deviated from the monastic code and then dispatched missionaries to various parts of Asia. According to this account, Ashoka's own son, who had become a monk, was dispatched to Sri Lanka; his daughter, a nun, followed shortly thereafter. Ashoka's edicts say nothing of a council of monks or the monastic involvement of his son and daughter, but even if the chronicle account is exaggerated, Ashoka certainly set a precedent for the relationship between government and Sangha.

The fall of the Mauryan dynasty in 185 B.C.E. did not greatly affect the fortunes of Buddhism. The Shungas, who succeeded the Mauryans in the northeastern heartland of the empire, were not positively disposed toward Buddhism, but neither did they cause significant disruption. Under the Satavahanas, who succeeded the Mauryans in the south, prosperous centers of Buddhism arose at Amaravati and Nagarjunikonda. By the third century C.E., Nagarjunikonda was a complex of twenty-seven monasteries and twenty *stupas*; inscriptions here record the gifts of members of the royal household as well as those of wealthy merchants. These centers were influential in spreading Buddhism to Southeast Asia.

The Indo-Greek kingdoms that succeeded Mauryan rule in the northwest supported Buddhism. King Menander (140–115 B.C.E.), the most famous of the rulers, is featured in the *Milinda-panha* (*Questions of Milinda*), a text on basic Buddhist teachings important to the Theravada tradition. In the text, Menander (Milinda) engages in a lengthy dialogue with a monk, Nagasena. At the end it is said that the king not only urged support for the Sangha, but he abdicated in favor of his son and became a monk.

The Greek kingdoms were succeeded by the rule of the Sakas and the Kushanas, invaders from Bactria (northeast Afghanistan) and Parthia (eastern Iran). The Kushanas, whose rule in the first and second centuries C.E. extended from northcentral India into central Asia (Afghanistan, Uzbekistan [USSR], and Chinese Turkestan), were avid patrons of Buddhism. During this period Buddhist monks and merchants established the tradition in central Asia and western China. King Kanishka (c. 78–101 C.E.) built *stupas* and monasteries; his coins bear the image of the Buddha. Fa-xian (Fahsien), a Chinese monk traveling in India around 400 C.E. remarks that the *stupa* built by Kanishka at Peshawar was the most magnificent of all the ones he saw on his journey. Images of the Buddha appear in the first century C.E., fashioned by artists at Mathura and in the Gandhara region, centers of Kushana rule. Traditional accounts say that Kanishka called a council of monks who recited and authorized a version of the *Tripitaka*.

Archeologists have uncovered the remains of monasteries and *stupas* dating from the second century B.C.E. The monasteries were either freestanding fired-brick structures or rock-cut caves. Typically, they consisted of cells for the monks surrounding a ceremonial hall. More than a thousand cave monasteries have been found, chiefly in western India, their construction dating from the second century B.C.E. to the ninth century C.E. A complete cave monastery consisted of a series of small rooms with rock beds and pillows, a pillared ceremonial hall, and a sanctuary, at the back of which was a *stupa* or *caitya* (a mound without a relic). The remains of great complexes of monasteries have been discovered at Sarnath, Kushinara, and Nalanda in the northeast, Sanchi and Mathura in central India, Peshawar and Taxila in the northwest, and Amaravati and Nagarjunikonda in the south.

The laity, especially wealthy merchants and rulers, built up monasteries in their desire for merit, not only the merit of financing construction, but also the whole range of merit-making opportunities made possible by the presence of a community of monks. From the Ashokan period on, the Sangha was drawn more and more into society. Rulers supported the monastic establishments as centers of culture and conveyors of blessing and protection to the state. Rulers and merchants' guilds as well as the common people made donations. Individual monks as well as monasteries received grants of land and/or portions of the income of a village to provide for their temporal needs. Along with the land they received the services of the tenants who worked the land. While laypeople were engaged to administer these properties, the senior monks in charge of monastery affairs in effect became landlords. In cases where the income from land and the donations of goods and money exceeded the needs of the monks, the monasteries built up a reserve of wealth that was then loaned to support local farmers or merchants.

The monasteries became centers of learning. The monks increasingly turned to scholarship and spent less time in meditation. They studied and taught a whole range of secular subjects as well as the Dharma. Some practiced medicine and gave astrological consultations. Even though Brahmanism had developed a whole range of life-cycle rituals, (birth, marriage, death, etc.), which the priests performed for members of the upper classes, Buddhist monks were often called upon to bless these occasions by chanting words of the Buddha. Very likely, they also performed funerals, memorial services, and house-blessing rituals for the lower classes. From ancient times to the beginning of the eighteenth century, the lay practice of religion in India was not exclusivistic; that is, people often participated in various aspects of different religions at the same time. We should not think of the laity of Brahmanism, Buddhism, and Jainism as competitive, or even clearly distinguished. King Ashoka is a good example of the laity in general. He declared himself a lay Buddhist, but he respected and supported the leadership of all sects and, on occasion, probably sponsored the performance of a Brahmanical fire ritual.

The *stupa* became a standard feature of the monastery environment, necessary to a sacred complex. Monks and nuns as well as laity contributed to the construction and upkeep of *stupas* and regularly walked around them and made flower offerings in prayer and meditation. Sanchi and Bharhut, in central India, were major complexes from 200 B.C.E. to 200 C.E. Inscriptions indicate that the remains of many renowned monks, including those of Sariputra and Maudgalyayana, were enshrined at Sanchi. The gateways to the large *stupa* at Sanchi are elaborately decorated with sculptures depicting scenes from the life of the Buddha. Prior to the first century B.C.E., there were no anthropomorphic portrayals of the Buddha. His presence was indicated by an empty space, footprints, a dharma wheel (see photograph on page 38), or the tree of enlightenment. Buddha-images originated at Mathura and Gandhara in northwest India and soon came to adorn the ceremonial hall of the monastery as well as the *stupas*.

The Rise of the Mahayana

The five hundred years from the fall of the Mauryan dynasty to the reunification of India under the Guptas was marked by the rise of

Mahayana, "Great Vehicle" Buddhism. The Mahayana was defined by the monks and grew out of doctrinal disputes rather than differences in monastic practice.

The monastic code was likely fully formulated by 300 B.C.E. and thereafter, apart from the differences of life-style between the minority forest-dwelling monks and the majority village-dwelling monks, there was general uniformity in monastic practice. Variant interpretations of the Buddha and his general teachings circulated from the earliest times; several schools of thought grew up in the Sangha without great consequence until the second century B.C.E. Then new **sutras** (discourses) appeared, purporting to be the "higher" teachings of the Buddha, hidden for a time and rediscovered. These sutras forced the drawing of doctrinal lines and the eventual division of the monks into adherents of either the Mahayana tradition or the more orthodox Theravada tradition, "The Way of the Elders."

The Theravada monks held to the view, represented in the early sutras, that the goal of the monastic life is arhatship, a goal achievable only by monastic discipline and not through the lay life. (The layperson may achieve heavenly bliss for a time, but will have to be reborn again in the human realm to pursue the monastic path). The *arhat* is one who has attained nirvana, that is, has extinguished all suffering by means of moral purity and insight and will not experience rebirth at the end of the present life. The elders believed that Buddhahood was unique to Gautama, at least within the present age of time, that Gautama had, in addition to *arhatship*, attained perfect knowledge by which to teach others the way to nirvana.

Mahayana monks submitted that the goal of the monastic life, a goal that could also be achieved in the lay life, is full Buddhahood. They criticized the pursuit of arhatship as a selfish pursuit and submitted that the complete extinction of suffering could only be achieved with the mental disposition of a **bodhisattva**. *Bodhisattvas*, "beings striving for enlightenment," strive on the monastic path or the lay path not for themselves, but for the welfare of others. They deny all self-interest, most of all interest in achieving nirvana. Even if they could have nirvana, they would refuse it to be born again and again for the sake of releasing others from suffering. *Bodhisattvas* are a force of compassion for the world. This ideal is clear, they argued, from the Buddha's own career, if not his early teaching. As the Buddha reveals in the "new" sutras, he has been on the *bodhisattva* path for eons and eons, striving to save other beings. And he will continue that striving—one should not think that with the death of Gautama, he became extinct. This apparent passing to nirvana, indeed also the achievement of enlightenment earlier, was only an appearance, an illusion to motivate others.

This Mahayana vision makes the "historical" Buddha a manifestation of a cosmic force, a transcendent principle and power. This principle and power is the pure Dharma, Dharma as the True Reality, that which pervades all, and is the true nature of every thing and being that exists. The Buddha of the new sutras reveals numerous other Buddhas, manifestations of Dharma, who preside over other universes in a vast reality and whose power radiates even into our world. The Buddha reveals countless *bodhisattvas*, striving in one state or another toward *bodhi* (enlightenment). What is important in this, according to the sutra, is not only that the way of the *bodhisattva* is the true way, but that the power of *bodhisattvas* is available for those in need. The *bodhisattva* ideal is double-edged—those who are ready should strive on the *bodhisattva* path; those who are not can call on the *bodhisattvas*' power. This ideal may have been influenced by developments in devotional Brahmanism/Hinduism, but most of all it is an elaboration of the early Buddhist teaching that the monk is a merit-field for others and the lay Buddhist belief in the power of relics of the saints.

This vision of the Buddhist way is called Great Vehicle, both because the ideal (Buddhahood) is great and because it is a way open to all (not just to monks), either by pursuing the *bodhisattva* path or by calling on the merit-power of the *bodhisattva* through prayer. Adherents of the Mahayana disparaged the Way of the Elders by calling it Hinayana, "Little Vehicle."

The emergence of Mahayana is marked by the appearance of a number of new scriptures between 100 B.C.E. and 200 C.E.: *The Sutra of the Lotus of the True Dharma* (*Sad-dharma-pundarika Sutra*), the *Vision of the Pure Land* (*Sukhavati-vyuha*), and *The Sutras of the Perfection of Wisdom* (*Prajna-paramita Sutra*). The *Lotus Sutra* reveals the Buddha as a cosmic being unbounded by time and space who exercises many skillful devices by which all beings may be saved and lauds the way of the *bodhisattva* over the one that leads to arhatship. The *Vision of the Pure Land* reveals the *bodhisattva* vows of the monk Dharmakara and describes the **Pure Land** paradise that Dharmakara establishes as the result of eons of striving. Dharmakara becomes known as **Amitabha Buddha**, "the Buddha of Endless Light." According to the sutra, his paradise in the western sphere of the cosmos can be reached by good deeds and meditation on Amitabha and his paradise or simply by praising his name over and over with full faith in his power.

The *Perfection of Wisdom* sutras set forth the higher wisdom of the Buddha, the wisdom of the accomplished *bodhisattvas* and transcendent Buddhas. This wisdom builds on the Buddha's teaching of "no-self." The so-called human person, which in reality is an aggregation of energies and processes arising and decaying every moment, is said to be "empty" (**shunya**), that is, empty of self, having no enduring nature. The same may be said of the entire phenomenal world; it is everywhere and completely in process and therefore devoid of an unchanging core. *Bodhisattvas* seek to realize the emptiness (*shunyata*) of self and world. They seek to dissolve the self that separates and alienates them in the life-flow. To dissolve self is to dissolve the distinctions that separate things and persons and cause suffering; it is to be one with each moment of life-flow as it occurs and, therefore, it is to experience the essential unity of life, the bliss of oneness. In the light of emptiness, *samsara*—the world of individual existence in bondage to karma—and nirvana are the same, that is, this very phenomenal world is nirvana when emptiness is realized.

These doctrinal differences did not notably alter the pattern of life of the Mahayana monks. They were no doubt reflected in their meditations, but Mahayana monks aspiring on the path of the *bodhisattva* did not become aggressive in social action. The *bodhisattva* saves by accumulating a store of merit that can be drawn on by others.

In the propagation of the Mahayana, its interpretation and transmission by individual masters took on more importance than in the Theravada. The most important of the early masters were Nagarjuna, c. 200 C.E., and the brothers Asanga and Vasubandhu, c. 400 C.E. Nagarjuna founded the Madhyamika ("Middle Way") school of interpretation and Asanga and Vasubandhu developed the Yogcara ("Practice of Yoga") school.

Monasteries came to be identified as either Mahayana or Theravada. They coexisted without strife, sometimes in the same monastery complex, and were equally appealing. Xuan-Zang (Hsuan-tsang), a Chinese Buddhist pilgrim to the major Buddhist centers in India from 630 to 644 C.E., estimates that in these centers there were a total of 115,000 Theravada monks in 2,000 monasteries and 120,000 Mahayana monks in 2,500 monasteries.

With the formulation of the Mahayana vision, the laity had more centers of power (the transcendent *bodhisattva*s and Buddhas) to appeal to in their prayers. Amitabha did not become popular in India, but rose to prominence in Chinese Buddhism. One of his close associates, the *bodhisattva* **Avalokiteshvara**, "The Lord Who (Kindly) Looks Down," the *bodhisattva* of infinite mercy, became an object of widespread appeal.

Final Flowering and Decline in India

The Gupta dynasty, 320–540 C.E. unified India once again and issued in the classical age of Indian culture. The Gupta kings were committed to Brahmanism/Hinduism, but they also patronized Buddhist institutions. A prime example is their construction of Nalanda, a great monastery complex, near their capital, Pataliputra. Nalanda became a full-fledged university offering a wide range of secular subjects as well as Buddhist studies; it attracted scholars from all over Asia. Construction began in the early fifth century. Xuan-Zang (Hsuan-tsang) describes its glory in the early seventh century:

> Six kings built as many monasteries one after the other, and an enclosure was made with bricks to make all the buildings into one great monastery with one entrance for them all. There were many courtyards, and they were divided into eight departments. Precious terraces spread like stars and jade pavilions were spired like peaks. The temple arose into the mists and the shrine halls stood high above the clouds . . . . Streams of blue water wound through the parks; green lotus flowers sparkled among the blossoms of sandal trees, and a mango grove spread outside the enclosure. The monks' dwellings in all the courtyards had four stories. The beams were painted with all the colors of the rainbow and were carved with animal designs, while the pillars were red and green . . . . In India there were thousands of

monasteries, but none surpassed this one in magnificence and sublimity. Always present were 10,000 monks, including hosts and guests, who studied both the Mahayana teachings and the doctrines of the 18 Hinayana schools as well as worldly books such as the Vedas and other classics. They also studied grammar, medicine, and mathematics . . . . The king gave them the revenues of more than 100 villages to support them, and each of the villages had 200 families who daily offered . . . rice, butter, and milk. Thus the students could have the four requisites (clothing, food, shelter, and medicine) sufficient for their needs without going to beg for them. It was because of this support that they had achieved so much in their learning.[14]

Relic worship grew to major proportions in the Gupta period in both monastic and lay Buddhism. The Chinese traveler Fa-xian (Fa-hsien; 400 C.E.) reports that at Peshawar the Buddha's begging bowl was enshrined. At Nagara, he found shrines for the Buddha's shadow, tooth, the flatbone of his skull, his sandalwood staff, and his robe. The Buddha's tooth-pick was found growing out of the earth where, it was said, he stuck it after cleaning his teeth. Fa-hsien found senior monks paying reverence at *stupas* for Sariputra, Maudgalyayana, and Ananda, and novices honoring a mound for Rahula (Gautama's son). There were *stupas* enshrining portions of the *Tripitaka*. He observed rulers making daily offerings at such shrines. At Shravasti Fa-xian (Fa-hsien) viewed a sandalwood image of the Buddha which he was told had been fashioned to symbolize the Buddha's presence when he went to the heavens to preach the Dharma to his mother. He was also informed that this was the pattern for all other iconic representations of the Buddha.

Beginning in the late fifth century, invading Huns sacked and burned many of the great monasteries of northwest India. They attacked the monasteries for their considerable wealth—donations of supplies, money, and images made from precious metals that had accumulated beyond the daily needs of the monks. Hsuan-tsang reports that some of these centers of Buddhism had been partially restored, but they would never return to their former status. Gupta power disintegrated in the mid-sixth century and the country returned to warring factionalism. Harsha reunited north India, 606–647 C.E., renewing support to traditional institutions; but thereafter the area was divided again into small kingdoms. The Palas, who came to power in northeast India around 750 C.E., strongly supported Buddhist institutions. They restored Nalanda, which had been destroyed at the death of Harsha, and built up two more monastery universities: Odantapura and Vikramasila. The Palas had extensive relations with kingdoms in Southeast Asia.

During the Pala period, a third "vehicle" of Buddhism, the **Tantrayana** ("the vehicle of [specialized] ritual"), came to maturity at Nalanda. Philosophically, the Tantrayana is consistent with the Mahayana and may be considered an offshoot. Its distinctiveness lies in its introduction into Buddhism of very old ritual techniques and Yoga practices. Numerous texts were produced by adherents of Tantrayana, but the true wisdom of the vehicle was known only to masters called *siddhas* ("Perfected Ones"). In contrast to the open transmission of knowledge in the Mahayana and Theravada traditions, the wisdom of the *siddha* was transmitted only in an intimate, one-to-one relationship with a carefully prepared disciple. *Siddhas* from Nalanda and the far northwest of India were responsible for the development of Buddhism in Tibet.

The monastic centers of Buddhism all across north India were utterly devastated by Muslim invaders in the late twelfth century. They were never to rise again. The wealth and power of their patrons was usurped by Muslim rule. With the death or dispersion of the monks, lay Buddhism could not sustain itself. Lay devotionalism was easily absorbed into Hinduism. Buddhism lingered, especially in south India, but by 1500 had passed from the Indian scene.

Beyond India

The Spread of Buddhism

As we have noted, the Buddha instructed his monastic disciples to go forth and preach the Dharma, "for the welfare of the many." The Sri Lankan chronicles record that following a great council of monks during the reign of Ashoka (269–232 B.C.E.), missionary monks were dispatched to various outlying areas of the subcontinent, Sri Lanka, and Southeast Asia. Even so, Indian Buddhism was not an aggressively proselytizing religion. By and large, Buddhism spread by the casual wanderings of monks and the travels of Buddhist merchants. Monks wandered eight months of the year in accordance with their discipline. The merchant class was strongly supportive of Buddhism from early times.

As in India, the growth and prosperity of Buddhism outside India was significantly the result of official patronage. Buddhism spread to the island of Sri Lanka off the southern tip of India in the latter half of the third century B.C.E. It may be that a diplomatic mission sent to the island by King Ashoka c. 247 B.C.E. encouraged its king to patronize Buddhism. If we accept the word of chronicles compiled in Sri Lanka in the fifth century C.E., missionary monks dispatched from Ashoka's capital (including Ashoka's son) converted King Tissa of Sri Lanka. According to the chronicles, Tissa built monasteries for monks and nuns ordained by the mission, enshrined the collarbone relic of the Buddha in a great *stupa*, and planted a slip of the bodhi-tree (the tree under which the Buddha achieved enlightenment) brought to the island from Bodh Gaya by the nun Sanghamitta, Ashoka's daughter. The chronicles also indicate that at the same time monks were sent to Sri Lanka, some were dispatched to Suvarnabhumi in Southeast Asia—probably what is today southern Burma and Thailand and the island of Sumatra. Indian traders established colonies across Southeast Asia as far as Vietnam and the islands of Indonesia beginning in the first century C.E. These colonies led to the rise of Indianized kingdoms in which Brahmanism as well as both Mahayana and Theravada Buddhism gradually rose to prominence.

Buddhism spread from northwest India into central Asia in the first century C.E. and from there "trickled" into western China. Kushana rule (first and second centuries C.E.) came to encompass the area from Banaras (northcentral India) west to include northern Afghanistan and north and northeast to include Uzbekistan (USSR) and Chinese Turkestan. The Kushana ruler Kanishka (c. 78–101) patronized Buddhism extensively. In the relative peace and prosperity of the Kushana period, monks and merchants carried Buddhism to central Asia and China along the trade routes. The remains of impressive *stupas*, cave monasteries, and freestanding brick monasteries and inscriptions and numerous Buddhist texts show that Buddhism thrived along the silk route for ten centuries. It was officially recognized in the kingdoms of Kashgar and Khotan (Chinese Turkestan) c. 150 C.E. Xuan-Zang (Hsuan-tsang), the seventh-century Chinese traveler to India, reports finding a hundred monasteries and five thousand monks at Khotan. Central Asian Buddhism provided most of the texts and scholars that spurred the development of Buddhism in China 300–600 C.E. Declining prosperity, the rise of Islam, and the declining fortunes of Buddhism in India and China lead to its disappearance in central Asia by 1000 C.E.

Chinese monks and diplomatic missions, perhaps on the model of Ashoka's "Dharma missions," carried Buddhism to Korea in the late fourth century C.E. Korean diplomatic missions introduced Buddhism at the Japanese court in the mid-sixth century. Thereafter, direct contact between Japan and China spurred the development of Japanese Buddhism. Buddhism reached Tibet from China in the seventh century. It was officially established by the Tibetan king Khri-srong (740–798), who invited a Mahayana monk from Nalanda to his court.

Integration

Except in the case of China, Buddhism was welcomed throughout Asia as the religion of a superior civilization. For Sri Lanka, Southeast Asia, and Tibet, the superior civilization was Indian civilization; for Korea, Vietnam, and Japan, it was Chinese civilization. Throughout Asia, Buddhism was accommodated to already established religions—spirit cults in Southeast Asia and Tibet, Confucianism and Daoism (Taoism) in China, and Shinto in Japan.

Buddhism appealed to a select few as a way of self-discipline and learning en route to nirvana. Its chief appeal to rulers as well as to the common people was as a religion of power in worldly affairs. Buddhist monks had a reputation not only for great learning, but also for extraordinary power over nature. It is said, for instance, that Ashoka's son, Mahinda, and his monastic companions flew through the air to Sri Lanka. The worship of the image of Buddha and his relics was considered a source of power for the present life as well as a means of gaining merit for the next life. The Buddha-image itself was believed to have power inasmuch as it was patterned after an image made during the lifetime of the Buddha and therefore qualified as a relic. Legend has it that the Chinese emperor Ming (ruling 58–75 C.E.) sent envoys of enquiry to India as the result of a dream in which he perceived a great golden Buddha. According to Japanese chronicles, in 538 C.E. a Korean ruler sent a mission to the Japanese court requesting military aid. The envoys presented the Japanese emperor with a gold-plated image of the Buddha, several Buddhist texts, and an exhortation that worship of the Buddha would result in prosperity in his kingdom. The Tantrayana *siddha* Padmasambhava was invited to Tibet in part for his reputation in exorcising evil spirits.

Initially, both Theravada and Mahayana traditions were practiced in Sri Lanka, Southeast Asia, and China. In time, the Theravada died out in northern Asia but came to be officially established in Sri Lanka and across the mainland of Southeast Asia (except in Vietnam) to the exclusion of the Mahayana. Tantric Mahayana developed as one of the several sects in Chinese and Japanese Buddhism; in Tibet, it eventually came to dominance.

Monks of Sri Lanka codified Theravada Buddhism by committing their traditions of what the Buddha taught to final written form during the first four centuries C.E. This authoritative text, written in a language called Pali, came to be known as the *Tipitaka* (Sanskrit, *Tripitaka*). Around 400 C.E., a monk named Buddhaghosa compiled and completed commentaries to the *Tripitaka* and a definitive summary of the teachings entitled *Visuddhimagga*, "The Path of Purification." After Buddhaghosa, the *Tripitaka*, his *Visuddhimagga*, and the *Milinda-panha* became the recognized standard of Theravada teachings and practices. Between the eleventh and the fourteenth centuries this Buddhism became officially established in the kingdoms of Burma, Thailand, Cambodia, and Laos.

The practice of Buddhism in Sri Lanka and Southeast Asia followed essentially the patterns established in India, with the exception that from its beginning in Sri Lanka, from the eleventh century in Burma, from the thirteenth in Thailand, and from the fourteenth in Cambodia and Laos, official patronage forged an intimate relationship between Sangha and government and led to the gradual disappearance or assimilation of other religions and the appearance of majority Buddhism. The Sangha prospered and at times significantly influenced the course of government but was also subject to close scrutiny and control by government.

Sri Lanka adopted the Indian caste system, and eventually casteism affected the Sangha as well as Sri Lankan society, dividing the Sangha into three distinct ordination lines. As the result of periods of south Indian rule and migrations from south India a large Hindu minority accumulated on the island and lay Buddhism gradually assimilated certain Hindu practices.

In Southeast Asian Theravada, ordination came to be seen as a rite of passage, an initiation into adult society, expected of all young men. Large numbers became monks for a short period of time; only a few undertook the monastic life as a lifelong commitment. Buddhism assimilated local spirit cults, just as it had assimilated the gods and spirits of popular religions in India.

In China, Buddhism had to compete with Confucianism and Daoism (Taoism), highly sophisticated and long-established religions. These religions were world affirming. Confucianism emphasized the family and harmonious relationships of loyalty and consideration—loyalty of son to father, wife to husband, subject to ruler; consideration of father for son, husband for wife, and ruler for subject. Buddhist monasticism devalued the family and placed loyalty to the discipline and the monastic community above that to the ruler and society in general. Daoism (Taoism) fostered introspection and nonconformism but in favor of light-hearted, easy flowing communion with nature rather than rigorous mental discipline. At the same time Confucianism valued learning (sageliness) and Daoism (Taoism) attributed extraordinary powers to one who lived in harmony with nature. Since learning and magical powers were key attributes of the accomplished Buddhist monk, the Chinese could appreciate the monk in spite of other areas of conflict. Furthermore, since the goal of Confucianism and Daoism (Taoism) was harmony in this world, the Buddhist belief in a heavenly rebirth gained by merit and the ultimate attainability of nirvana added new dimensions to Chinese religious life.

Confucianism was the established religion of the Han dynasty (202 B.C.E.–220 C.E.). In the period of disunity and disfavor toward Confucianism following the fall of the Han (300–600), monastic Buddhism gained general acceptance and official support. A census of 517 C.E. indicates that there were then thirty thousand monasteries and two million monks and nuns. The pattern of monastic life was much like that of Indian Buddhism with the major exception that the monasteries were self-sustaining through land grants and the monks had much less daily intimacy with society because they did not go out for food. Also, the monastic communities largely arose focused on individual master monks; each community was made up of a master and his disciples. This arrangement, which was a tendency in Indian Mahayana Buddhism, was accentuated in China by the Confucian and Daoist (Taoist) ideal of sageliness. By way of contrast, in Theravada Buddhism the focus was on the community itself, in which each monk had a common status.

Mahayana Buddhism in India tolerated great diversity of thought without dividing into distinct sects. In China, from the sixth century on, a variety of sects took shape, each appealing to one or another of the Mahayana sutras. The two sects that gained the greatest popularity and came to have the largest impact on Japanese as well as Chinese Buddhism were the Chan (Ch'an), or "Meditation" sect (Jap., **Zen**) and the Jing-tu (*Ching-t'u*), or "Pure Land" sect (Jap., Jodo).

The early monks of China, influenced from India, emphasized scholarship and were perhaps somewhat lax in keeping the ancient monastic code. Chan (Ch'an) monks downgraded concern with textual learning and translation and emphasized discipline and above all meditation. They withdrew into the mountains, where they developed a variety of new techniques for achieving insight. They also innovated by introducing manual labor as part of the monastic discipline. Following Mahayana teaching, particularly *The Sutras of the Perfection of Wisdom*, they taught that this very concrete world is the realm of enlightenment. Influenced by Daoism (Taoism), they taught that ordinary, mundane activity could be the occasion for enlightenment.

Other Chinese monks had discovered *The Vision of the Pure Land* sutras which praised Amitabha Buddha (Chin., *A-mi-duo-fo [A-mi-to-fo]*) and his Pure Land paradise. Amitabha and his Pure Land were the object of meditation in Indian Buddhism. The Chinese master Tan-luan (T'an-luan) (476–542) interpreted the Pure Land scriptures to say that one could attain the Pure Land after death simply by reciting the name of Amitabha in the manner: *nă-mo ă-mi-to-fo* "Reverence to Amitabha Buddha." He taught that by such recitation alone, without meditation or any particular discipline, and by Amitabha's grace, one could gain the Pure Land paradise; once in the Pure Land, nirvana would be easy to attain. In a relatively brief time, this teaching attracted thousands of persons, both monks and laity, to faith in Amitabha Buddha in the hope of being reborn in his paradise.

Along with Amitabha Buddha, the *bodhisattvas* Avalokiteshvara and **Maitreya** also became popular objects of worship in China. Avalokiteshvara (Chin., *Guan-yin* [*Kuan-yin*] was accommodated to pre-Buddhist religion by identification with a goddess who, like Avalokiteshvara, was believed to have power over fertility. Lay Buddhism in China did not develop the distinctive style in which it was integrated with the life of the monks that it developed in India, Sri Lanka, and Southeast Asia. It came to consist largely of merit making by gifts to the monasteries and worship of Buddhas and *bodhisattvas* alongside of the worship of pre-Buddhist gods and spirits.

Japanese Buddhism developed on the Chinese model, with the notable exception that, from the thirteenth century on, Pure Land (Jap. *Jodo*) Buddhism gave up monasticism and began functioning with a married clergy. In Japan, Buddhism was accommodated to a native spirit cult called Shinto, "The Way of the Spirits." A division of labor developed making Shinto priests responsible for worldly affairs, such as consecrating marriage, and Buddhist monks responsible for funeral rites.

Had Buddhism not become established outside India, it may well have died out after the destruction of the great monastic centers in India around 1200. Sri Lankan monks preserved the texts and traditions of the Theravada and Chinese and Tibetan monks preserved the literature and traditions of the Mahayana.

In Tibet, Buddhism took shape primarily under the influence of Indian Mahayana masters and at the height of the popularity of Tantric Mahayana. As in other parts of Asia, monks and monasteries played a key role in its establishment and growth. However, both traditional Mahayana monk scholars and Tantric wonder-working *siddhas* were instrumental in this process; and some of the *siddhas*, like Padmasambhava, were householders (noncelibate). Tantric *siddhas* did not necessarily adhere to the monastic code followed by Mahayana and Theravada monks; their teachings were passed to disciples in a private relationship rather than through ordination by a body of monks. Tantric practices came to dominate Tibetan Buddhism under the leadership of both monastic and nonmonastic masters (**lamas**). The recognition of different lineages of masters divided its practice into six distinct schools or sects.

Tibetan Buddhism developed two unique features: first, the institution of the reincarnation of *lamas*, based on the belief that each successive head *lama* in a given lineage is a reincarnation of the previous head lama in that lineage; and second, *lama* rule over Tibet. The Mongol ruler of China in the thirteenth century appointed a *lama* as regent over Tibet. In 1656, Tibet came under the direct rule of a *lama* with the title of **Dalai Lama** or "Ocean Lama." The current Dalai Lama lives in exile in northwest India.

Beyond Asia

European presence in Asia from 1500 on brought Buddhism to note in the West. European scholars, some of whom became devotees, assisted in the revival of Buddhism in Sri Lanka and its reintroduction into India and founded Buddhist societies in England and Germany. Chinese and Japanese immigrants transplanted the faith in Hawaii and the western United States. An influx of Japanese and Tibetan monks and scholars in this century has produced sizable communities of Buddhists throughout the United States.

CHAPTER III

Buddhism as a Unified System of Beliefs and Practices

We have seen how Buddhism developed from the life and teachings of Siddhartha Guatama into a religion practiced worldwide. Now let us look at this religion as a fully developed system functioning in the modern world. As in the historical survey, our focus will be Asian Buddhism, both Theravada and Mahayana. With respect to the Mahayana, we shall specifically consider the Zen and Pure Land Buddhisms of Japan.

Overview

All that we are is the result of what we have thought: it is founded on our thoughts, it is made up of our thoughts. If a man speaks or acts with an evil thought, pain follows him, as a wheel follows the foot of the ox that draws the carriage. If a man speaks or acts with a pure thought, happiness follows him, like a shadow that never leaves him.[15]

The "*result* of what we have thought" is karma. Buddhism defines the world in terms of karma. Karma manifests itself as a multitude of life forms, each with its distinctive characteristics and potential, each in its appropriate sphere or environment according to its merit-status. Karma causes suffering; it causes relative happiness; and it causes ultimate happiness—release from suffering, nirvana.

The resources for shaping good karma, which results in worldly prosperity, favorable rebirth, and nirvana, are the Buddha, the Dharma, and the Sangha. These Three Treasures are the source of self-power to those who actualize them through a life of self-discipline. They are power to be shared with those who respect them, have confidence in them, and worship them. The Buddha is a heroic example for those who seek self-power. He is a reservoir of merit for those who need to rely on the power of another. The Dharma is wisdom-power or enlightenment-power to those who comprehend it. It is a force of healing, protection, and blessing to those who invoke it. The Sangha is an instrument of enlightenment and nirvana to those who commit themselves to its discipline. It is a reservoir of merit for those who respect and materially support it.

The Theravada and Mahayana interpretations of the Three Treasures, each in its own way, give emphasis to both foci of the Buddha's life and teaching—self-power through self-discipline and shared power by the conjunction of compassion and devotion. Charity, moral discipline, meditation, and worship are the means of actualizing the power of the Three Treasures, that is, making and sharing merit in the production of good karma and the attainment of worldly prosperity, enlightenment, and nirvana. These means dictate a ritual ordering of individual, familial, and community life.

The World as Constituted by Karma

There is no story of the first or primal creation in the annals of Buddhism. Buddhists, like Hindus, taking their cue from the repeating phases of the sun and moon in relation to the earth and the ever-repeating cycles of growth and decline in nature, think of time and space as without beginning or end and incessantly pulsating in lesser and greater cycles. The material universe repeatedly issues forth from a state of latency, expands to a peak, and then declines to a state of rest once again, much as the moon appears, phases from new to full, and then goes back to new. Of course, the life span of a manifest universe, 432 billion years (a *maha-kalpa*), is enormously greater than the 30-day "life" of a moon. Within the great span of time of the *maha-kalpa,* the universe pulsates in lesser phases of 432

million years (a *kalpa*), each of which is constituted of four ages
(*catur-yuga*). A universe is made up of one billion world systems,
each of which consists of an earth with heavens above and hells
below.

While they recognize these great cycles of time and the numerous
world-cycles, the teachings of Buddhism focus on the repeated cycling (*samsara*) of life forms in this world system by reason of karma. Karma, the force or energy created by human thoughts, words,
and deeds, causes the various life forms that inhabit our world system—their physical and mental capacities, sex, and social circumstances. There are gods who reside in heavens above the earth; humans, demons, hungry ghosts, and animals who live on or near the
earth; and hell dwellers whose abode is below the earth. Karma is of
two kinds: meritorious (*pun*ya, or "good," karma) and demeritorious (*papa,* or "bad," karma). Merit results in pleasure, demerit in
pain. Merit and demerit are accumulated in human existence. Their
effects must be experienced, if not in the present life, then in another. Human beings who die with greater merit than demerit are
reborn as gods or again as humans. Those with greater demerit than
merit are reborn as demons, hungry ghosts, animals, or inhabitants
of hell. The life of a god is one of great pleasure; that of a human,
mixed pleasure and pain; and that of demons, hungry ghosts, animals, and hell dwellers, great pain. Thus, it is desirable to gain heav-
en, or at least rebirth in a human form of high status and potential.
But, even heavenly existence comes to an end when merit is exhausted; these beings must then revert to human status, or if they carry
sufficient demerit from their former human existence, a lower form
where they experience the results of this demerit. Therefore, the ultimate goal of the practice of Buddhism is freedom from karma and
rebirth, freedom from suffering.

The resources for merit and through it for the attainment of
heaven and nirvana are the Three Treasures or Jewels: the Buddha,
the Dharma, and the Sangha. Faith or confidence in the Three Jewels is the foundation of the practice of Buddhism. It is expressed by
the chanting of the Threefold Refuge:

> Reverence to the Lord, the Holy One, the Perfectly
> > Enlightened One!
> I take refuge in the Buddha!

I take refuge in the Dharma!
I take refuge in the Sangha!

Full faith in Buddha, Dharma, and Sangha is the mark of conversion, the assurance that one will never again be born in a form of life lower than human. The content of this confidence is defined in an early formula:

> The elect disciple is in this world possessed of faith in the Buddha—believing the Blessed One [*bhagavan*] to be the Holy One [*arhat*], the Fully-enlightened One [*sammasambuddha*], Wide, Upright, Happy, World-knowing, Supreme, the Bridler of men's wayward hearts, the Teacher of gods and men, the Blessed Buddha.
>
> He (the disciple) is possessed of faith in the *Dharma*—believing the truth to have been proclaimed by the Blessed One, of advantage in this world, passing not away, welcoming all, leading to salvation, and to be attained to by the wise, each one for himself.
>
> And . . . he is possessed of faith in the *Sangha*—believing the multitude of the disciples of the Blessed One who are walking in the four stages of the noble **Eightfold Path,** the righteous, the upright, the just, and law-abiding—believing this church of the Buddha to be worthy of honor, of hospitality, of gifts and of reverence; to be the supreme sowing ground of merit for the world . . .[16]

"Taking refuge" in the Buddha, Dharma, and Sangha has two levels of meaning. It means following the example of the Buddha by practicing the Dharma—giving gifts (*dana*), cultivating morality (*sila*), and striving for wisdom (**prajna**) through meditation (*samadhi*). It also means relying on the power (merit) of the Buddha, Dharma, and Sangha, which is actualized by prayer, offerings, and ritual incantations. The Three Jewels are resources for worldly prosperity as well as for the achievement of nirvana.

The Buddha

The Buddha is the great teacher and example of one who attains nirvana for those treading the path that he revealed. At the same time, by his meritorious deeds, purity, wisdom, and compassion, he is a reservoir of power for those in need.

The Buddha is the Holy One (*arhat*)—he has conquered all lust, anger, and delusion, dispelled all sensuous desire, all yearning for personal existence, and all ignorance. He is the Perfectly Enlightened One—he has knowledge of his former lives, knowledge of the sufferings of other beings, knowledge of anything he wishes to know.

> Now, someone, in things never heard before, understands by himself the truth, and he therein attains omniscience, and gains mastery in the powers. Such a one is called a *sammasambuddha*.[17]

By his holiness and perfect enlightenment, he is the Blessed One, the Lord and Teacher of all beings—he has power over all realms of life and the compassionate skill to deliver all beings from suffering. He is

> abounding in wisdom and goodness, happy, with knowledge of the worlds, unsurpassed as a guide to mortals willing to be led, a teacher for gods and men, an exalted one, a Buddha. He, by himself, thoroughly knows, and sees as it were face to face, this universe—includ-

The Buddha, in meditation posture, amidst the ruins of an ancient monastery at Anuradhapura, Sri Lanka.

ing the worlds above of the gods, the Brahmas, and the Maras [forces of death]; and the world below with its *samanas* and *brahmanas,* its princes and peoples—and having known it, he makes his knowledge known to others.[18]

He is the Tathagata, the one "Thus-come" or "Thus-gone." He has come and gone the way of a Buddha: he has come, accumulating great merit through many lives; he has gone beyond the physical and mental characteristics that define and limit other beings:

> In the world with its devas [certain of the gods], Maras and Brahmas, amid living beings with recluses and Brahmins [Brahmanas], devas and mankind, the Tathagata is the victor unvanquished, the absolute seer, self-controlled. Therefore is he called Tathagata.[19]

A Tathagata has ten powers by which he comprehends all causes and effects, the nature and destiny of all beings. A *brahmana,* seeing the footprints of the Buddha with their thousand-spoked wheel markings, exclaimed: "Indeed, how wonderful and marvelous—it cannot be that these are the footprints of a human being." Coming to the Buddha he inquired, 'Is your Lord [Are you] a god, an angel, a demon, or a human being?" The Buddha responded that he was none of these; rather he was a Buddha. All the characteristics by which he would be a god, an angel, demon, or man had been extinguished.

> Just as a . . . lotus, although born in the water, grown up in the water, when it reaches the surface stands there unsoiled by the water—just so, brahmin, although born in the world, grown up in the world, having overcome the world, I abide unsoiled by the world. Take it that I am Buddha[20] . . .

Great Events

The story of the Buddha, as it came to be told from the second century B.C.E., is a story of heroic conquest, compassionate service, and the exercise of impressive power. Representing the Buddha as an example of perfection in self-control and self-knowledge and the magnificence and power of a perfected being, it is an inspiration toward faith, charitable deeds, and morality and a model for the monastic life. It portrays a wondrous being who is supremely confident, completely in control not only of himself but of the physical environment and all of the gods, spirits, and powers honored and feared by the people of the Buddha's time. The great events of the story are the birth of Gautama at Lumbini, his renunciation of worldly things at the age of twenty-nine, his enlightenment at Gaya six years later, his first sermon at the deer park near Banaras—"setting in motion the wheel of the Dharma"—and his death at Kushinara at the age of eighty. These events are the final effects of long strivings—the strivings of more than five hundred lives.

The Buddha's pilgrimage to enlightenment began "one hundred thousand cycles vast and four immensities ago," when Sumedha, a wealthy and learned *brahmana,* happened upon a Buddha by the name of Dipamkara. Sumedha, dissatisfied with life and overwhelmed by the serenity of Dipamkara, vowed to undertake the discipline by which he too would become a Buddha. Thereafter, he was known as a *bodhisattva,* "a being striving for enlightenment."

When Sumedha died, the force of his deeds and his vow to seek enlightenment caused the birth of a new form—a body and consciousness appropriate to these accumulated life-energies. In this form and again and again in hundreds of rebirths, sometimes human form and sometimes nonhuman, the *bodhisattva* strove to achieve ten perfections: perfection in morality, renunciation, courage, patience, truthfulness, resolution, good will, equanimity, wisdom, and charity. For example, as a rabbit, he showed supreme charity by offering his body on the fire to provide food for a hungry *brahmana:*

> There came a beggar, asked for food;
> Myself I gave that he might eat.
> In alms there's none can equal me;
> In alms have I perfection reached.[21]

As a great bull elephant, he was pierced in the navel by a hunter's poisoned arrow but showed no antagonism toward the hunter. Indeed, as he slowly died, he graciously assisted the hunter in removing his tusks. Finally, as Prince Vessantara, the *bodhisattva's* last life but one, he manifested supreme perfection in charity, giving away not only his material wealth, but his beloved wife and children.

The Magnificent Conception and Birth

At the death of Prince Vessantara, the *bodhisattva* was born among the gods where he reflected on the circumstances of his upcoming final birth. Concurrently, on the earth in the Shakya capital city of Kapilavastu, Queen Mahamaya, sleeping, dreamed of being carried off to a golden mansion on a silver hill somewhere in the Himalayas. There, laid out on a couch, assisted by several angelic beings, she experienced the arrival of a great white elephant. The elephant, bearing a lotus in its trunk and trumpeting loudly, circled her couch three times and entered the side of her body. Thus was Gautama conceived, and the entire cosmos responded:

> Now the instant the Future Buddha was conceived in the womb of his mother, all the ten thousand worlds suddenly quaked, quivered, and shook. . . . An immeasurable light spread through ten thousand worlds; the blind recovered their sight; . . . the deaf received their hearing; the dumb talked; . . . rain fell out of season. . . . In the mighty ocean the water became sweet . . .[22]

Having awakened and reported her dream to King Suddhodana and the wise men of the court, she was informed by the wise men that she would bear a son who would either become a universal monarch or a Buddha.

When pregnancy was nearing its term, Queen Mahamaya set out for the home of her parents, there to give birth. Labor pains came upon her en route, near the village of Lumbini. Withdrawing to a grove of Sal trees blooming out of season, she gave birth to the child while standing, holding onto a branch of a tree. The child emerged from her side, pure and sparkling, and fell into a receiving net held by several of the gods. Bouncing up from the net, the well-formed child came down on the ground and, taking seven steps, shouted, "I am the greatest of all beings. This is my last birth!"

Prince Gautama was born on the full moon of the month of Vaisakha (April–May). (His renunciation, awakening, and death will all occur on this same day of the year.) His body bore the thirty-two marks of greatness, some of which were golden skin with a hair to each pore and so smooth that dust would not cling to it, netted hands and feet, and thousand-spoked wheel designs on the soles of his feet. Asita, a wandering ascetic, wept upon seeing the child because he realized that the child would become enlightened and teach others, but only after his (Asita's) own death. Queen Mahamaya died seven days after Gautama's birth and was reborn in one of the heavens of the gods.

Still a baby, the child was left seated beneath a great tree during a plowing festival; there he entered upon meditation and experienced successively four states of trance. He will reflect back on this incident as he sits just prior to final awakening.

The Great Renunciation

The young Gautama showed skill in all the martial arts and great promise toward becoming a ruler. He married Yashodhara at age sixteen. However, even though he was surrounded by lovely female servants and enjoyed all the physical comforts, he was unhappy. According to the biographies, at age twenty-nine, riding near his father's palace, Gautama saw persons suffering from disease and old age; then, he happened upon a funeral procession. Informed by his charioteer that disease, old age, and death are common to all people, he became despondent and returned to his room for deep reflection. Upon observing a serene wandering monk, he vowed to renounce his princely status and go forth into the homeless life in search of a cure for suffering and death. Not long before this decision, Yashodhara bore him a son, Rahula (literally, "fetter").

Late one night, setting surrounded by the exhausted bodies of dancing girls and servants with spittle running from their mouths as they slept sprawled on the floor, he experienced utter revulsion. Kissing his sleeping wife and child, he took his horse and favorite servant and started for the gate of the city. The Great Renunciation had begun! The gate to the city was securely locked, but the "spirits," cheering on Gautama's renunciation "for the welfare of gods and men," opened it with ease. Going forth, he stopped near the river, cut his hair with his sword, exchanged his princely attire for the simple clothing of a passing hunter, and dismissed his horse and servant.

Gautama joined the *samanas* inhabiting the forests of Koshala and Magadha. He practiced Yoga successively under the guidance of two well-known *samana* masters but found no deep satisfaction. He then spent several years with five companions practicing severe asceticism, attempting to starve the body into submission by extreme fasting. On the verge of death and having only enhanced suf-

The Bodhi Tree—tree of enlight-enment—at Bodh Gaya in northeast India; believed to be the tree under which Gautama attained final awakening. The Mahabodhi temple in the background dates from the twelfth century. The stupas in the foreground enshrine relics of saints.

fering rather than having conquered it, he again wandered alone, finally settling in a grove near the village of Gaya.

Seated beneath a great fig tree, his body glowing with a golden aura, he received the first solid food since breaking his fast. A young woman, Sujata, who believed she had been blessed with a good husband and a male child as the result of a prayer beneath the great tree, came to make an offering of fine food to the tree. She made her offering to Gautama, thinking him to be the spirit of the tree. Gautama took the food; he bathed at the river, ate, and cast the food bowl into the river where it floated upstream, a sign that he was destined that day to become a Buddha. At nightfall, the night of the full moon in Vaisakha (April—May), the same night on which he was born, he seated himself again beneath the tree facing east, determined not to rise until he had achieved true insight:

> Let my skin, and sinews, and bones become dry, and welcome! And letall the flesh and blood in my body dry up! But never from this seat will I stir, until I have attained the supreme and absolute wisdom![23]

Then came Mara, the Lord of Death, and his hosts of demons

personifications of all the desires and ego-ridden satisfactions of human life. Exclaiming, "Prince Siddhartha is desirous of passing beyond my control, but I will never allow it," Mara arrayed his army for battle.

> Mara's army extended in front of him for twelve leagues, and to the right and to the left of him for twelve leagues, and in the rear as far as to the confines of the world, and it was nine leagues high. And when it shouted, it made an earthquake-like roaring and rumbling over a space of a thousand leagues. And the god Mara, mounting his elephant, which was a hundred and fifty leagues high and had the name "Girded-with-mountains," caused a thousand arms to appear on his body, and with these he grasped a variety of weapons.[24]

Mara tempted Gautama with lovely women and positions of wealth and power. Failing to dissuade him from his discipline, Mara showered fierce storms upon him—rain, hot rocks, flies, and wind. Each successive shower was transformed into harmless flowers as it came near the pure and powerful *bodhisattva*. Finally, in desperation Mara questioned Gautama's perfection, taunting him as being alone and without a witness to his achievement. Gautama shifted the fingers of his right hand to point to the ground and silently called upon the earth itself to witness to his perfection. Mother Earth bellowed forth, "I bear you witness," and Mara and his hosts were utterly dismissed. The entire cosmos of nonhuman beings—gods, spirits, snakes, birds, and so forth—acclaimed his victory:

> The victory now hath this illustrious Buddha won!
> The Wicked One, the Slayer, hath defeated been![25]

The Setting in Motion of the Wheel of the Dharma

The Buddha remained seven weeks in the vicinity of the great tree, savoring his insight and pondering whether it would be profitable to try to teach others what he had discovered.

> Through painful striving have I gained it,
> Away with now proclaiming it;
> By those beset with lust and hate

Not easily is this teaching learnt.
This teaching, fine, against the stream,
Subtle, profound, and hard to see,
They will not see it, lust-inflamed,
Beneath the mass of darkness veiled.[26]

Seeing that the Buddha was "inclined to remain in quiet," Brahma, himself, lord of the gods of the Brahmanical pantheon, came down to persuade him to go forth and teach:

Lord, may the Blessed One preach the doctrine! May the perfect One preach the doctrine! There are beings whose mental eyes are darkened by scarcely any dust; but if they do not hear the doctrine, they cannot attain salvation. These will understand the doctrine. . . . The Dhamma [Dharma] hitherto manifested in the country of Magadha has been impure, thought out by contaminated men. But do thou now open the door of the Immortal; let them hear the doctrine discovered by the spotless one! . . . Look down, all-seeing One, upon the people lost in suffering, overcome by birth and decay. . . . Arise, O hero; O victorious One! Wander through the world, O leader of the pilgrim band, who thyself art free from debt. May the Blessed One preach the doctrine; there will be people who can understand it![27]

Receptive to Brahma's plea and encouragement, the Buddha decided to go to Banaras. He had first thought to enlighten his former teachers, but the gods informed him that they had died. He then saw, with his "divine, clear vision" his former companions in asceticism, dwelling at a deer park near Banares. He decided that they should be the first to hear his teaching, and so proceeded to Banaras. There, his former companions greeted him with great respect and he delivered his first sermon, called "The Setting in Motion of the Wheel of Dharma." In it he taught the Middle Way consisting of the Four Noble Truths:
1. The truth of the existence of suffering;
2. The truth of the cause of suffering;
3. The truth of the cessation of suffering; and
4. The truth of the path that leads to the cessation of suffering.
One after the other, the companions, "having understood the Dharma, . . . having dispelled all doubts, . . . having gained full

knowledge,'' asked the Buddha to receive them as disciples. In a short time, all five attained the status of *arhats*—those free of all attachment to the world.

Feats of Ministry

Many extraordinary feats are attributed to the Buddha. He exorcised disease-causing spirits from a city; he preached while walking in the sky. He instantaneously quieted a mad elephant; he outwitted the great magicians of his time. In one of the more spectacular events of his ministry, the Buddha ascended into the heavens to preach the Dharma to his mother where she resided among the gods. After three months he descended to the earth triumphantly on a jeweled staircase accompanied by the Brahmanical gods Brahma and Indra. When the Buddha goes into the village for alms

> . . . gentle winds clear the ground before him; the clouds let fall drops of water to lay the dust in his pathway, and then become a canopy over him; other winds bring flowers and scatter them in his path; elevations of ground depress themselves, and depressions elevate themselves; wherever he places his foot, the ground is even and pleasant to walk upon, or lotus flowers receive his tread. No sooner has he set his right foot within the city gate than the rays of six different colors which issue from his body race hither and thither over palaces and pagodas, and deck them, as it were, with the yellow sheen of gold, or with the colors of a painting. The elephants, the horses, the birds, and other animals give forth melodious sounds; likewise the tom-toms, lutes, and other musical instruments, and the ornaments worn by the people.[28]

The Great Decease

In his last year, traveling north from Rajagriha, the Buddha fell ill with dysentery. A short time later, this condition was aggravated by a meal of dried boar's flesh he received from Cunda, a blacksmith. He retired to a grove near the village of Kushinara. There, lying on his side, he gave final instructions to Ananda about the monastic life, authorized the ordination of one last disciple, and received the Malla people of Kushinara who had come to pay their respects. As he lay dying, flowers fell from the sky and heavenly music sounded; the area was crowded with the gods—for twelve leagues around the grove "there was no spot in size even as the pricking of the point of the tip of a hair which was not pervaded by powerful spirits." Finally, with the words: "To everything that arises, there is cessation; work out your salvation with diligence!" he passed in and out of a series of states of deep concentration and expired.

> When the Blessed One died there arose, at the moment of his passing out of existence, a mighty earthquake, terrible and awe-inspiring; and the thunders of heaven burst forth.[29]

Malla chieftains prepared the body for cremation. They were unable to move it or to set it afire without first apprehending the will of the spirits. When the cremation was completed, the fire was extinguished by a flow of water from the sky. After some debate, the remains were distributed to eight parties who, upon returning to their native places, enshrined them in memorial mounds (*stupas*).

The great events of the Buddha story are well known to every devotee. The Buddha's former lives, especially the one as Prince Vessantara, are remembered in acts of charity. His birth, enlightenment, and death are celebrated as events of great power by festivals, pilgrimages to Lumbini and Bodh Gaya, and the building of *stupas*. The Great Renunciation is reenacted at every ordination to the monastic order. Various mishaps of life are commonly referred to as due to the attack of Mara, and they are faced with the confidence of knowing that the Buddha conquered Mara. The incident of the Earth Goddess witnessing to the Buddha's merit is appealed to in every act of transferring or sharing merit in the Theravada tradition. The whole story of the Buddha concretely illustrates the integration of gods and spirits into the Buddhist worldview and the subordination of these powers to the power of the Buddha. The gods honor and serve the Buddha and the spirits are vanquished by his power; these episodes provide inspiration for many of the rituals of daily life.

Two Visions of the Buddha

Theravada Buddhism affirms the Buddha as a unique being of the present age of time (indefinite in length). He stands in a line of Buddhas, the enlightened ones of other times, each of whom brought the Dharma. He has achieved a status that will not be achieved by others in this age. He has come and gone, leaving the Dharma as a guide by which others may attain arhatship, the extinction of suffering but not full Buddhahood. This view is exemplified by remarks attributed to the Buddha just after his great awakening. On the road to Banaras, Gautama met an ascetic, Upaka, who, noticing his serenity and pure and bright complexion, asked what teacher and doctrine the Buddha followed. The Buddha replied:

> I have overcome all foes; I am all-wise; I am free from stains in every way; I have left everything; and have obtained emancipation by the destruction of desire. Having myself gained knowledge, whom should I call my master? I have no teacher; no one is equal to me; in the world of men and of gods no being is like me. I am the holy One (*Arhat*) in this world, I am the highest teacher, I alone am the Perfectly Enlightened One (*sammasambuddha*); I have gained coolness and have obtained nirvana. To found the kingdom of truth (*dharma*) I go to the city of the Kashis (Banaras).[30]

The Buddha foretells the coming of the Buddha for the next age, Maitreya, who now resides in the Tusita heaven awaiting his time for birth in the human realm. Theravada Buddhists occasionally appeal to the power of Maitreya as well as to that of the Buddha Gautama. Maitreya, of course, is "alive" in the world system and may be prayed to directly; even so, residing as he does in another realm, his presence is distant and his power not particularly related to everyday matters of human life. Gautama has come and gone, but his power is close at hand and can be easily brought to bear on mundane affairs. It resides in the Dharma which is mediated by the monks, and in the *stupas,* bodhi-trees, and images, which are still "hot" by their association with the Buddha or his remains.

In the Theravada, the concept of *bodhisattva* ("A Being of [i.e., destined for] Enlightenment") is not central to the doctrine of Buddhahood. It is applied to the many lives through which the Buddha strove toward Buddhahood. The designation does not especially emphasize striving for the sake of others, nor is it applied to anyone other than the Buddha, former Buddhas, and Maitreya, the one to come. It is not used in reference to the Buddha's disciples. It is significant to the Theravada that the Buddha proclaimed the Dharma for the world, but this is not the central purpose of his striving as a *bodhisattva*. The Buddha's power for others, like that of the monk, is incidental to his striving for nirvana.

In the Mahayana the concept of the *bodhisattva* is central and has the meaning (as, in fact, exemplified by the lives of the Buddha) of a being striving toward enlightenment not for his or her own sake, but for the sake of others. It also has the meaning of a being who has attained enlightenment but forgoes nirvana in order to deliver others from suffering. A Buddha, for eons prior to perfect enlightenment (Buddhahood) and thereafter, that is, even as a Buddha, is essentially A Being for Others. Further, he has not come and gone, but exists eternally, emanating merit (goodness and truth) throughout the cosmos.

In the discourse known as *The Sutra of the Lotus of the True Dharma,* the Buddha reveals his transcendent nature as everlasting: "Father of the world, the Self-born One, Healer, Protector of all creatures,"who attained perfect enlightenment eons and eons ago, but out of compassion for his children takes form again and again to educate them and bring them to nirvana. Like a father who offers his children splendid bullock-, deer-, and goat-drawn carts to lure them out of a burning house, to which they are oblivious by their play, the Tathagata offers people various vehicles (teachings) by which each of them, according to his or her capacity, may attain to nirvana. Like a father who, separated from his son for many years, employs various skillful devices by which to bring his son to an awareness of his inheritance, the Tathagata, Father of the world, exercises various means by which to save suffering beings. Since their parting, the father has become rich and powerful, the son poor and destitute. The father remembers and longs for his son; the son has long since forgotten his father. When the father happens to see his son, his impulse is to run to him and embrace him as a son, but he realizes that the son, in his destitute state, would be unable to comprehend that he is really the heir to great wealth. Instead, the father sends servants to offer the son work in the stables. After a time, the father disguises himself and works alongside of his son, getting acquainted and encouraging the son to look upon him as if he were his father. Eventually the father bestows his wealth upon the son, revealing to him his true nature.

As the father in the parable disguises himself to work alongside of his son, so the Tathagata makes appearance among people as **Shakyamuni** ("The sage of the Shakya Tribe"—a title for Gautama Buddha preferred in the Mahayana) and skillfully plays out the drama of renunciation, the attainment of enlightenment, the wandering teaching, and final decease:

> The force of a strong resolve which I assumed is such . . . that this world, including gods, men, and demons, acknowledges: Now has the Lord Shakyamuni, after going out from the home of the Shakyas, arrived at supreme, perfect enlightenment . . . at the town of Gaya. But . . . the truth is that many hundred thousand myriads of kotis [ten millions] of eons ago I have arrived at supreme, perfect enlightenment. . . . I . . . created all that with the express view to skillfully preach the Dharma. . . . Without being extinct, the Tathagata makes a show of extinction, on behalf of those who have to be educated.[31]

The transcendent, formless Tathagata is called the Dharma-kaya, the "Dharma body" or "Dharma principle." Shakyamuni is the Nirmana-kaya or "Appearance body," the Dharma temporarily taking form in the phenomenal world. The Dharma principle also manifests or takes form in celestial realms or Buddha-lands. This is the Sambhoga-kaya, "Enjoyment body"—the form by which various Buddhas enjoy themselves and are enjoyed by the happy beings who inhabit their realms.

The Mahayana envisages an enormous cosmos made up of numerous universes, many of which are "Buddha-fields," paradises, each presided over by a Buddha whose merit assists suffering beings. Also inhabiting these realms are countless *bodhisattvas* striving to relieve suffering and enjoying the vision of the Buddhas and the hearing of the Dharma that constantly emanates from these Buddhas. To understand this phenomena of numerous Buddhas and *bodhisattvas,* we must have in mind not only that the one Buddha-truth or Dharma princple takes many forms, but also that the goal of the practice of the Mahayana is not arhatship, in the sense of individual extinction, but bodhisattvahood and Buddhahood.

Amitabha Buddha (Chin. *A-mi-duo-fo* [*A-mi-to-fo*]; Jap. *Amida Butsu*), "The Buddha of Endless Light," presides over Sukhavati, "The Pure or Happy Land," in the western region. Eons ago he was the monk Dharmakara who, like the Buddha Shakyamuni, heard the preaching of a Buddha and vowed to strive as a *bodhisattva* to achieve full Buddhahood. He vowed to strive to accumulate the merit necessary to create the most magnificent paradise, a land "prosperous, rich, good to live in, fertile, lovely, . . . rich with mani-fold flowers and fruits, . . . adorned with silver and gold gem trees," a land rich with every conceivable food, to be consumed simply by the thought of it. There would be no physical or mental pain and only gods and humans would reside there. By Dharmakara's vow, men and women could be reborn in this paradise by good deeds and meditating on Amitabha; they may even be received there by simply hearing Amitabha's name and keeping it firmly in mind for one night. Having arrived in the Pure Land, they may remain there in-definitely or, if they wish, pass easily to nirvana. Striving for many eons, Dharmakara attained his goal and now resides in Sukhavati as Endless Light and Endless Life (Amitayur).

Other Buddhas have no personal history like that of Amitabha; they are essentially personifications of characteristics of enlighten-ment, ruling the spheres of the cosmos. Akshobhya, "the Imper-turbable," presides in the east. Vairocana, "the Illuminator" (Jap. *Dainichi,* "Great Sun"), reigns in the center. Ratnasambhava, "the Jewel-born," presides in the south, and Amoghasiddhi, "the Un-failing Success," reigns in the north.

Among the celestial *bodhisattvas,* the most powerful and gra-cious is Avalokiteshvara (Chin. *Guan-yin* [Kuan-yin]; Jap. *Kan-non*), "the Lord Who (Kindly) Looks Down from Above." Origin-ally male, he is designated female in China and Japan. He resides in Amitabha's Pure Land as chief attendant of the Buddha. Having strived on the *bodhisattva* path for hundreds of eons, he

> possesses the perfection of all virtues, and beholds all beings with compassion and benevolence, he, an ocean of virtues, Virtue itself, . . . is worthy of adoration.

He saves those in dire trouble, who merely think of Him:

> If one be thrown into a pit of fire, by a wicked enemy, . . . he has but to think of Avalokiteshvara, and the fire shall be quenched as if sprin-kled with water. . . . If a man delivered to the power of the execution-

ers, is already standing at the place of execution, he has but to think of
Avalokiteshavara, and their swords shall go to pieces.[32]

He grants the wish of women who pray to him for children.

The Dharma

Dharma has the dual sense of "the doctrine" and "the path" taught
by the Buddha; and the latter is most important. Doctrines merely
point to that which is to be realized experientially. The power or
merit of Dharma lies in the practice and realization of it in one's life.
It also resides in the mere sound of the Dharma, the energy of the
Buddha-word, when ritually chanted. The word of the Buddha, like
the Buddha-name (e.g., Amitabha, above), is charged with the
merit of the Budha and is powerful simply as sound, apart from the
meaning of the word.

The Dharma to Be Realized

The core of the Dharma is the Four Noble Truths:
1. There is suffering (**duhkha**);
2. Suffering is caused by desire;
3. The cessation of desire results in the cessation of suffering (nirvana); and
4. There is a path that leads to the cessation of desire.

These truths are not theories—the result of philosophical specula-
tion—nor are they the content of a divine revelation. They were realized experientially by the Buddha through moral discipline and
meditation—rigorous self-analysis. They are the conclusions of a
physician, rather than the reasonings of a metaphysician or the vi-
sions of a mystic. The physician experienced disease (suffering), experientially isolated its cause (desire) and therefore its cure (cessation
of desire), and took the medicine (the Path) by which he definitively
conquered the disease. Buddhism takes a psychological approach to
reality, describing the world in terms of a depth analysis of personal
experience. It begins with an existing state of affairs—the personal
experience of physical and mental suffering—and looks for a solution to this undesirable state of affairs not in manipulating the natu-

ral environment or human society, but in examining the feelings and thoughts of the sufferer. The fact of suffering is to be comprehended; the cause of suffering is to be abandoned; the cessation of suffering is to be realized; and the path that leads to the cessation of suffering is to be practiced.

A man asked the Buddha a series of abstract questions: "Is the world eternal or noneternal? Are the soul and the body the same or different?" and the like, saying that if he could answer these questions satisfactorily, the man would become his disciple. The Buddha replied that the questioner was like a person wounded with a poisoned arrow who wanted to know who shot the arrow, the assailant's village, caste, family, and so on, before being willing to have his wound attended to. The Buddha's point was that the wounded man's questions, like philosophizing about life in general, draw attention away from the existential, "brute" fact that there is suffering, that it has a cause and a cure. The Dharma is not a general theory about life but a practical and personal discipline by which one may realize the nature and extinction of suffering.

SUFFERING

> This is the Noble Truth of Suffering: birth is suffering; decay is suffering; illness is suffering; death is suffering; presence of objects we hate is suffering; separation from objects we love is suffering; not to obtain what we desire is suffering. In brief, the five aggregates which spring from grasping, they are suffering.[33]

All religions wrestle with the finitude—the impermanence and imperfection of human existence. In a word, Buddhism describes this problem as suffering (*duhkha*). Being born is suffering; growth is suffering; experiencing disease is suffering; growing old and dying is suffering. Subtler than physical pain is the suffering of dissatisfaction, the unhappiness occasioned by not having what we want and having what we do not want. There is anxiety (mental suffering) even in the experience of pleasure and satisfaction—the knowing or at least apprehension that it will not last. There is fear of failure, loss of status, loss of self-worth, loss of loved ones, loss of property. Deep down, there is a vague and gnawing anxiety about death—not only the prospect of life ending but of ultimate meaninglessness. It is anxiety about death that motivates human striving, that makes the world run.

To describe existence as suffering implies more than simply physical pain. *Duhkha* signifies a state of being "ill-at-ease, insecure, unsatisfied." It identifies life as impermanent and characterized by constantly changing personal identity (**anatman**). Everything that exists is transitory, momentary, subject to constant change. With respect to the natural world, this is a fact confirmed by modern science. We used to speak of particles in motion—matter and energy; now, we speak of energy fields. What is functionally a solid object is, in fact, a process identified by reference to molecules, electrons and protons, motons, and so on, which themselves are not solid, but processes, patterns of interacting energies.

What is true of nature at large is also true of human existence. Buddhism identifies the human being as interacting moments of material form, sensations, consciousnesses, perceptions, and volitions (acts of will). These energy patterns are called the Five Aggregates. These aggregates are no more solid than molecules and electrons. Everything that a person is or experiences can be described in terms of the interaction of these five phenomena.

The material sense organs (eye, ear, nose, tongue, body, and mind) come into contact with sense objects, giving rise to sensations, which are either pleasant, unpleasant, or neutral;

> From sensation arises consciousness, awareness of an object;
> From consciousness arises perception, the identification of the object;
> From perception arises volition, an act of will with reference to the object.

I touch a finger to a table; a sensation (smoothness, hardness, etc.) arises from material contact. From the sensation a consciousness arises: the awareness of the object that is smooth and hard. This touch consciousness causes the perception of a table and stimulates a decision to sit on the table. As there are six organs of sense and six kinds of sensory objects—sight, sound, smell, taste, touch, and thought—so there are six kinds of sensations, perceptions, consciousnesses, and volitions. They are all momentary, incessantly rising and passing.

There is no unchanging personal identity, no self (*atman*) apart from the constantly changing aggregates. This is the teaching of "no-self" (*anatman*): not no self at all, but no permanent, underlying selfhood or soul. The interplay of the aggregates creates the illusion of a self—an agent underlying and experiencing materiality, sensation, consciousness, perception, and volition—just as a point of light moving in a circular pattern creates the illusion of a solid circle of light. In fact, there is no such self—a person is process, a constant becoming.

> In the absolute sense, beings have only a very short moment to live, life lasting as long as a single moment of consciousness lasts. Just as a cart wheel, whether rolling or whether at a standstill, at all times only rests on a single point of its periphery: even so the life of a living being lasts only for the duration of a single moment of consciousness. As soon as the moment ceases, the being also ceases. For it is said: "The being of the past moment of consciousness has lived, but does not live now, or will it lie in future. The being of the future moment has not yet lived, nor does it live now, but it will live in the future. The being of the present moment has not lived, it does live just now, but it will not live in the future.[34]

The aggregate energies arise and decay in serial succession, the cessation of one moment causing the rise of the next, the self being born and dying from moment to moment.

DESIRE

Thus, life is impermanent; in particular it is without unchanging personal identity and characterized by the experience of physical and mental suffering. Having identified a condition, the physician/psychoanalyst inquires into the cause of that condition. He or she asks, "What is the cause of suffering?"

> This is the Noble Truth concerning the Origin of Suffering: verily, it originates in that craving which causes rebirths, is accompanied by sensual delight, and seeks satisfaction now here, now there; that is to say, craving for pleasures, craving for existence, craving for nonexistence.[35]

It is easy to see how desire or craving causes mental suffering. If a person wants something that cannot be attained, there is mental stress. If something or someone a person is emotionally attached to is taken away, there is the anguish of loss. We can understand how desire causes physical suffering, if craving leads a person into a situation in which injury occurs. It is not so easy to understand how desire causes the physical suffering inflicted by, say, an earthquake or by another person where one is an innocent bystander. Much of the suffering of the human condition is inherent in the impermanence of that condition. But Buddhism submits that desire is the cause of the very existence of a human being. There are no innocent bystanders. This is explored and explained by what is called the Wheel of Becoming—the wheel of life based on the principle of **dependent origination.**

The wheel identifies causal patterns, factors linked in dependence, one giving rise to another. Together they constitute what is called *samsara,* an "endless cycling," marked by birth, death, and rebirth. *Samsara* is symbolized by the demon Mara (literally, "death") holding the wheel in his grasp. In general, three factors of ill—greed, hatred, and delusion, symbolized by the cock, the snake, and the pig at the wheel's center, perpetuate *samsara.* They cause humans to be reborn in realms of punishment—as demons, animals, hungry ghosts, or denizens of hell. Those who strive to conquer the three ills are reborn again as humans or in heaven as gods. The outer ring breaks down the twelve factors that characterize human life from moment to moment and in the past, present, and future.

Reference to desire is only a simple, convenient way of referring to a whole complex of continuously arising and ceasing states discovered by meditative self-analysis. Desire (8) arises in a person dependent upon sensations (7), which arise from contacts (6)—physical and mental impressions occasioned by the existence of sense organs and mind (5). The sense organs and mind are the instrumentalities of a body (4) that has come to exist as the result of a life-force called consciousness (3). This life-force is what we associate with the interaction of sperm and egg, which then is to be thought of as materializing itself, "growing itself" a body with a brain, nervous system, and sense organs in the mother's womb. Such an organism, through contact with itself, other organisms, and physical

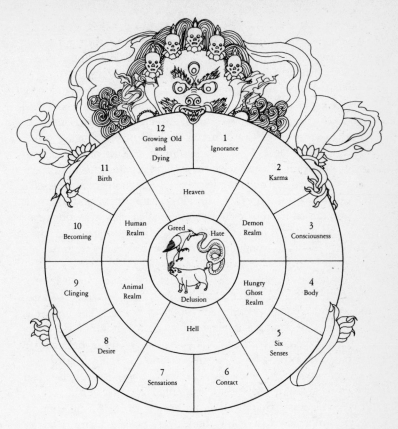

The Wheel of Becoming

objects, experiences sensations (7) that give rise to desires (8). Desires lead to clinging (9)—attachment to things and persons—which perpetuates and progressively complicates ongoing life or the process of becoming (10). It is desire for sensory pleasure, desire for life, or even desire for death that perpetuates life.

These eight factors (3—10) describe present life, but they do not arise out of nothing. Life does not begin at birth or even at conception. The life-force of birth-consciousness (3) is the result of acts of will (karma) (2) that occurred in a previous existence. These acts of will arose as the result of ignorance (1) of the true nature of reality.

Thus, two factors in the past (ignorance and karma) gave rise to the eight factors that characterize the present. Likewise, the eight factors of present life result in the life-force of yet another, future life—birth (11) (rebirth) and more growing old and dying (12).

Thus, desire is bound up with a fundamental delusion that continually expresses itself as an individual personality, with body and mind interacting with sense objects, striving for satisfaction of desires. Desire gives rise to attachment or grasping—a clinging to life, to self—which causes continued becoming, rebirth, and from birth decay and death. These twelve elements in a causal chain of dependent arising may be taken to describe any one moment in a person's life (a moment of ignorance, volition, consciousness, and so on) or the progression from past life (life essentially characterized by ignorance and volitions) to present life (life in the Five Aggregates, characterized by desire, clinging, and constant becoming) to future life (birth and continued growing old and dying).

The first two noble truths, then, describe the common human situation—suffering as the result of desire. If one asks, "Whence did desire, ignorance, birth, and selfhood begin?" The answer is both that a beginning is imperceivable and the inquiry is not fruitful. It is imperceivable because a being caught up in becoming is unable to see beyond his or her own creation. It is not fruitful to so inquire, because the question is abstract, purely speculative, and does not effectively relate to the existential situation of suffering, its cause, and destruction. Seeking an answer to such a question is, again, comparable to a man wounded by a poisoned arrow who demands to know who shot it before he will have his wound attended to. Dharma addresses itself to the immediate human predicament—there is suffering, it has a cause, it can be destroyed, and there is a path by which to destroy it.

If one asks, "If there is no self, no soul, what is reborn? What experiences desire and the rest?" the answer is that it is simply the Five Aggregates that are constantly arising and ceasing, like a flickering flame. Each flicker is momentary, arising out of the previous flicker and giving rise to the next by its own extinction. Birth and death occur every moment in what we call life; the final flicker of the present gross body is no different from any one moment in the life of this body.

THE CESSATION OF DESIRE

> This is the Noble Truth concerning the Cessation of Suffering: verily, it is passionlessness, cessation without remainder of this very craving; the laying aside of, the giving up, the being free from, the harboring no longer of, this craving.[36]

Stated simply, the third noble truth is that if desire (the whole complex chain of becoming) is the cause of suffering, then the cessation of desire is the cessation of suffering. Cessation of suffering is nirvana, "blowing out," "extinction" of the flame of greed, hate, and delusion.

> Enraptured with lust (*raga*), enraged with anger (*dosa*), blinded by delusion (*moha*), overwhelmed, with mind ensnared, man aims at his own ruin, at the ruin of others, at the ruin of both, and he experiences mental pain and grief. But if lust, anger and delusion are given up, man aims neither at his own ruin, nor at the ruin of others, nor at the ruin of both, and he experiences no mental pain and grief. Thus is nirvana visible in this life, immediate, inviting, attractive, and comprehensible to the wise.[37]

Nirvana is freedom from future rebirth, old age, and death. It may be said to be blissful, but not in any sense of worldly pleasure or, for that matter, any pleasure defined by other than the absence of suffering. The aggregates may linger, but not with any sense of self, and when one's accumulated karma finally flickers totally out, one cannot be said to have gone anywhere—to a heaven, for instance. The aggregates simply cease, go out, not to arise again.

> Mere suffering exists, no sufferer is found; The deed is, but no doer or the deed is there; Nirvana is, but not the man that enters it; The Path is, but no traveler on it is seen.[38]

THE PATH

Nirvana is to be realized by treading the Eightfold Path:

> This is the Noble Truth concerning the Path which leads to the Cessation of Suffering: verily, it is this Noble Eightfold Path, that is to say,

right views, right intent, right speech, right conduct, right means of livelihood, right endeavor, right mindfulness, and right meditation.[39]

The Eightfold Path consists of three dimensions:
> Wisdom (*prajna*), which consists of right views and right intent;
>
> Morality (*sila*), which consists of right speech, conduct, and livelihood;
>
> Mental Discipline (*samadhi*), which consists of right endeavor, right mindfulness, and right meditation.

Wisdom as right views is, to begin with, an intellectual acceptance of the Four Noble Truths. In the end, it is the full realization, the full penetration of these truths. Right intent is intent free of sensuous desire, ill will, and violence. Positively stated, it is goodwill (*maitri*) toward all living beings, compassion (*karuna*) for all suffering beings, sympathetic joy (*mudita*) in the success and happiness of other beings, and equanimity (*upeksha*) in all states of affairs.

Morality may be summarized by the **Five Precepts:** not to lie, not to kill, not to steal, not to engage in illicit sex, and not to partake of intoxicating drink. Right speech is abstaining from lying, slander, harsh or malicious talk, and idle gossip. Right conduct is abstaining from taking life, stealing, and unlawful sexual activity. Right livelihood is abstaining from making a living by activities that bring harm to other beings—trafficking in weapons or alcoholic drink, the killing of animals, prostitution, and the like.

In the Buddhist ethic and in accordance with belief in the Law of Karma, concern for the welfare of others is essentially concern for one's own welfare. Wrongdoing is not sin in the sense of being subject to judgment and punishment by another being; it is self-inflicted punishment by the fact of its bringing suffering upon oneself, if not immediately, in later life or some future existence. This is not to say that some immoral acts are not subject to punishment under civil or monastic law; but it is to say that the motivation for behavior should come from within rather than from fear of punishment by society.

A monk is walking along the narrow embankment that separates the muddy rice fields. He is pushed off into the mire by a careless man hurrying to pass him. The man rushes on without saying anything or stopping. Another man, seeing this incident, runs up to help the monk out of the muddy field. Back on the embankment, the monk quietly proceeds, without comment to or about either of the other men's actions. When asked about his behavior by the second man, who desires praise for his assistance, the monk calmly replies, "I have learned to be even-minded in all circumstances; you and the other man have your reward."

Mental development must proceed hand in hand with morality to produce right views and right intent. Right effort is essentially the exertion to rid oneself of unwholesome states of mind and to cultivate wholesome states of mind. It, like all other dimensions of the Path, critically depends upon right mindfulness:

> This is the sole way, monks, for the purification of beings, for the overcoming of sorrow and lamentation, for the destroying of pain and grief, for reaching the right path, for the realization of Nirvana, namely the four Foundations of Mindfulness. What are the four? Herein (in this teaching) a monk dwells practicing body-contemplation on the body, ardent, clearly comprehending the mindful, having overcome covetousness and grief concerning the world; he dwells practicing feeling—contemplation on feelings, . . . mind-contemplation on the mind, . . . mind-object—contemplation on mind-objects . . .[40]

Mindfulness is the heart of Buddhist meditation. It is practiced by giving close attention to the functioning of the body, the feelings, the mental processes, and conceptual patterns like those found in the teachings of the Buddha. In practicing mindfulness of breathing, for example, one should sit with the body erect and mind alert and simply watch one's breathing:

> Breathing in a long breath, he knows "I breathe in a long breath"; breathing out a long breath, he knows "I breathe out a long breath"; breathing in a short breath, he knows "I breathe in a short breath"; breathing out a short breath, he knows "I breathe out a short breath."[41]

By directing the mind solely to the breathing over longer and longer periods of time, one becomes more and more keenly aware of this bodily process, calming the body and objectifying the process so as to depersonalize it—to strip it of any sense of ego or selfhood.

We may see more clearly how mindfulness affects ego if we consider the mindfulness of feelings, such as a feeling of anger. Turning one's attention to the anger feeling itself and away from its object or activity that might follow from anger, one "defuses" or depersonalizes the feeling by seeing it for what it essentially is—just another psychophysical process that now disperses as quickly as it has arisen. This practice of mindfulness is to be extended to all bodily functions, all feelings (pleasant as well as painful), all states of mind, and all particular ways of thinking about body and mind. Once the mind is trained in solitude, one is able to practice mindfulness in the course of ordinary daily activity—mindfulness of walking, sitting, eating, and so on. In every activity one undertakes one should carefully consider and clearly comprehend its purpose relative to one's goals and its suitability or potential effectiveness toward achieving those goals; then one should apply mindfulness to the action while engaging in it, gradually stripping it of all sense of self, all personal attachment.

> In looking forward, or in looking round; in stretching forth his arm, or in drawing it in again; in eating or drinking, in masticating or swallowing, in obeying the calls of nature, in going or standing or sitting, in sleeping or waking, in speaking or in being still, he keeps himself aware of all it really means.[42]

Mindfulness enhances one's capacity to live in accord with the moral precepts. It builds insight toward wisdom (right view and right intent) by allowing one to more and more thoroughly realize the impermanence, suffering, and impersonality of life, the cause of suffering, the cessation of suffering, and the path that leads to the cessation of suffering—in short, to realize the Four Noble Truths and to see things as they really are.

The capacity for mindfulness may be enhanced by developing right concentration. The purpose of practicing concentration is to quiet or tranquilize the mind by experiencing radically altered states of consciousness, states of deep absorption. To accomplish this one focuses the mind on one or another of some forty recommended objects of concentration, suitable to one's ability and personal disposition. For instance, a beginner sitting quietly may take a circle of light red clay the size of a dish as an object. By focusing upon it intensely, the person produces a mental image, which then becomes the object—one that he or she may hold before the mind even while interrupting the sitting for some other activity. By occupying the mind entirely with this mental object, one excludes all other sensory-mental awareness and enters the first of a series of trance states:

> Detached from sensual objects, detached from unwholesome states of mind, the monk enters the first absorption, which is accompanied by thought-conception and discursive thinking, concentration, rapture and joy.[43]

With the passing away of thought conception and discursive think-ing, the person enters a second absorption characterized by concen-tration, rapture, and joy. The third absorption is characterized by only concentration and joy, and the fourth simply by equanimity. One dismisses each successive absorption by practicing mindfulness on its contents—seeing there impermanence, suffering, and imper-sonality. By the insight of this mindfulness, one may gain special powers:

> Being one he becomes many; having become many, he again becomes one; he appears and disappears; unhindered he goes through walls, fences and mountains as through the air; he submerges and emerges in the earth as in water; without sinking he walks on the water as on the earth; cross-legged he flies through the air like a winged bird; he touches and strokes with his hand the sun and the moon . . .[44]

The Buddha discouraged his disciples from using these powers, even though much is made of them in the literature and the Buddha himself is portrayed as having used them on several occasions. The experience of such power should serve only to confirm the level of attainment in concentration. They are incidental to the progress to-ward enlightenment; exercising them may lead one astray from in-sight to nirvana; they should not be employed by way of impressing others as to the validity of the teaching.

There are other powers that are directly instrumental to cessation of desire and enlightenment. Having attained the highly rarefied levels of consciousness through concentration, one may experience superhuman hearing and sight: the divine ear, the capacity to see into other persons' minds; and the divine eye, the ability to perceive one's own former lives and the sufferings and births of other beings. Finally, through applying mindfulness to each of the four absorptions, one may attain the knowledge-power by which to extinguish the three cankers (*asavas*): sensuous desire, the desire for existence, and ignorance. This is nirvana, deliverance from birth and death.

The progress from mindfulness to nirvana is described as a sevenfold attainment: the attainment of mindfulness leads to the investigation of reality, to the rise of extraordinary energy, rapture, tranquility, concentration, and finally equanimity.

Progress on the Path is also described as gradually overcoming ten binding obstacles: the belief in self, doubt, attachment to rules and ritual, sensuous craving, ill will, the craving for rebirth among the gods of subtle form, the craving for rebirth in the formless realms, conceit, restlessness, and ignorance. The one who has overcome the first three obstacles has become a Stream-entrant, that is, one who has definitively entered the stream flowing toward nirvana. A Stream-winner dying at this level of attainment will never again be reborn in a realm lower than the human. A disciple who is nearly free of obstacles four and five—sensuous craving and ill will—becomes a Once-returner, that is, one who will return to this world only once more and in that life attain nirvana. The disciple who is totally free of the first five obstacles is a Non-returner, that is, one who will be reborn in a realm higher than human and will reach nirvana from that realm. One who conquers all ten obstacles attains nirvana in this very life; he or she becomes an *arhat*, a Holy One.

THE PATH IN VARIOUS TRADITIONS

The Mahayana develops the teaching of "no-self." To say that there is no unchanging personal identity is to say that a life form is empty (*shunya*), devoid of an essential nature; it is incessant process or energy flow. This is true of things as well as persons. To see the world as it really is, the goal of moral discipline and meditation, is to realize its emptiness (*shunyata*). This does not mean to see that the world does not exist; it means to see that everything that exists exists in a relation of dependence and, therefore, in an essential unity.

Nirvana is not a negation of the world, but a seeing of the world such as it is, without the imposition of personal selfhood upon it.

The unity of life is called Buddha-nature; thus, it is said that everything has Buddha-nature and to realize the essential unity of life is to realize one's Buddha-nature. This is the perfection of wisdom (**prajna-paramita**).

Logically, emptiness is the necessary implication of the dependent origination of all phenomena. If, in a series of factors identifying a phenomenon (e.g., the twelve factors of the Wheel of Becoming), the first factor causes the second, the second causes the third, and so on to the last factor, which causes the first, then the existence of any factor depends upon another factor—it has no existence of its own, no existence apart from relationship; it is empty of self-nature; it has only relational nature.

The larger implication is that the existence and well-being of a life form is dependent upon the existence and well-being of every other life form. A life form has true existence only by existing in harmony with and for the welfare of other life forms. A *bodhisattva* exists solely for the sake of others.

The *bodhisattva* strives on the same Eightfold Path as those who seek arhatship. The key difference is two fold: first, the *bodhisattva* strives for the perfection of wisdom that is the perfect enlightenment of a Buddha and not simply cessation of suffering (nirvana); second, the *bodhisattva* vows to strive for the release from suffering of all beings and vows to forego personal nirvana in order, life after life, to share his or her merit with others. The hallmark of the *bodhisattva* is compassion.

Monks striving on the Theravada path are a field of merit for others, although their intent is the conquest of suffering in their own lives. *Bodhisattvas* realize that in a universe in which life forms are totally interdependent there is no release for one without the release of all. They see also that the means must be compatible with the end. If the end is selflessness, then the means must be an emptying of self for others, existing only for others. Those who strive only for their own happiness will never attain selflessness.

Bodhisattvas strive for six perfections (*parami*): perfection in giving, morality, patience, vigor, meditation, and wisdom. It is the same path as that taken by Theravada monks, but the intention is different. After many lives of deeds of charity, they give without any thought of self or reward. Their giving is informed by the realization of the emptiness of self and others and, therefore, their identity;

their giving is perfected. Then they are able to arouse "the thought of enlightenment" (*bodhi-citta*), from which they will never thereafter lapse. They vow to strive for perfection in morality, patience, and so on, for the sake of all beings. It is the force of this vow that distinguishes their striving from that of those striving to become *arhats;* indeed, their energy is the much greater because they strive for others and not for self.

> The *bodhisattva* is endowed with wisdom of a kind whereby he looks on all beings as though victims going to the slaughter. And immense compassion grips him. His divine eye sees . . . innumerable beings, and he is filled with great distress at what he sees, for many bear the burden of past deeds which will be punished in purgatory, others will have unfortunate rebirths which will divide them from the Buddha and his teachings, others must soon be slain, . . . others have gained a favorable rebirth only to lose it again.
>
> So he pours out his love and compassion upon all those beings, and attends to them, thinking, "I shall become the savior of all beings, and set them free from their sufferings."[45]

Zen monks pursue a different discipline of meditation than that prescribed by the Eightfold Path. In the Soto (Zen) tradition, simply sitting (Jap., *zazen*) without focusing the mind anywhere is the basic technique:

> To study the way of the Buddha is to study your own self. To study your own self is to forget yourself. To forget yourself is to have the objective world prevail in you. To have the objective world prevail in you, is to let go of your "own" body and mind as well as the body and mind of "Others."
>
> In the pursuit of the Way the prime essential is sitting. . . . Just to pass the time in sitting straight, without thought of acquisition, without any sense of achieving enlightenment.[46]

This sitting is intended to have the same result as mindfulness meditation—a progressive emptying of the mind resulting in immediacy with the flow of life. Rinzai Zen advocates a more active meditation, active both in the sense of focusing the mind on an object rather than simply sitting passively and in the sense of doing such meditation in the course of ordinary daily activity as well as in formal sitting. The meditation object, called a *koan,* is a riddle or puzzling story given the student by the master that defies intellectual solution. Persistent meditation upon its meaning produces mental exhaustion and occasions a sudden, intuitive insight—a disjunction in the flow of ordinary, purposeful thought. Solving the *koan* may be assisted by a well-timed shout or blow of the hand or a stick administered by the master.

The Power of Dharma as Sound

Every word of the Buddha is charged with merit. Certain of his discourses, by reason of the occasion on which they were given or by the fact that they summarize the essence of the teaching/truth, are considered to be especially powerful. In the Theravada tradition, these are called *parittas,* "protective blessings." In the Mahayana, they are called **dharanis,** "those (words) which hold (power)."

In the *Vinaya* collection of the *Tripitaka,* there is report of an occasion on which a monk was bitten by a snake and died. The Buddha reportedly said:

> I allow you, O monks, to make use of a safeguard [*paritta*] for yourselves for your security and protection, by letting your love flow out over the four royal breeds of serpents. And thus, O monks, are you to do so:
>> I love live things that have no feet, the bipeds too I love. I love four-footed creatures, and things with many feet. . . . Let no footless thing do hurt to me, nor thing that has two feet . . .
>> Infinite is the Buddha, infinite the Dharma, infinite the Sangha. Finite are creeping things. . . . Made is my safeguard, made my defense. Let living things retreat, whilst I revere the Blessed One . . .[47]

This authorization of the use of *paritta* applies only to protection from wild animals and it assumes that the one using the formula is, indeed, full of love (***maitri,*** "loving-kindness"). That is to say, the power of the exhortation lies in the merit of the exhorter and not simply in the formula as a magical spell or charm. These and other words of the buddha came to be used in a variety of circumstances (to promote general prosperity as well as specific protection) and only by persons who were assumed to be highly meritorious. In the Theravada tradition the *paritta* is chanted by monks or exmonks, and in the Mahayana by monks or masters, whether monastic or lay.

The *Mangala Sutra*, "the Discourse on Auspiciousness," is the *paritta* most frequently used in Theravada practice. In it the Buddha summarizes the moral principles of lay Buddhism. This *paritta* is invoked on all occasions in which there is merit making and sharing beween monks and laity. The *Angulimala paritta,* on the other hand, is used to allay the pain of childbirth. It is the word of the Buddha to the monk Angulimala, who was desirous of easing the pain of a woman giving birth:

> Go to the place and say, "I have never knowingly put any creature to death since I was born; by the virtue of this observance may you be free from pain."[48]

In the twenty-second chapter of the Mahayana *Sutra of the Lotus of the True Dharma,* it is said that anyone who hears this sutra "will produce an accumulation of pious merit the term of which is not to be arrived at even by Buddha-knowledge."[49] *The Sutra of the Heart of the Perfection of Wisdom,* which summarizes the wisdom on emptiness, is also considered a most powerful *dharani.*

The Sangha

In the Theravada, the Sangha is the community of monks. It may also have the more limited sense of "the community of saints"—all those who, through the ages, achieved arhatship and are, like the Buddha fit objects of prayer and meditation. In the Mahayana, the Sangha includes all who are striving in the way of the Buddha, lay devotees as well as monks.

Those who undertake the way of the monk are ordained to a life of poverty and strict discipline. Theravada monks are ordained by a body of senior monks, a minimum of five for the novitiate ordination and ten for the higher ordination. They vow to keep the Ten Precepts:

1. Not to take life;
2. Not to lie;
3. Not to steal;
4. Not to engage in sexual activity;
5. Not to drink alcohol;
6. Not to take food from noon to the next morning;
7. Not to adorn their bodies with anything other than the three robes;
8. Not to participate in or be spectator to public entertainments;
9. Not to use high or comfortable beds;
10. Not to use money.

In addition, those of the higher ordination commit themselves to keep the 227 rules of the monastic code (*Pratimoksha*) and to regularly (twice monthly) recite these rules and confess any infraction thereof in the company of other monks. They are to keep to themselves in study and meditation, except when they go into the village or city to receive food offerings or perform a merit ceremony for the laity.

The preferred and usual time for ordination is in May and June, just prior to the rainy season. On the Theravada mainland of Southeast Asia, it is customary for all young men to receive the lower or novitiate ordination and many also undertake the higher ordination. Monks are free to leave the monastic life at any time. The great majority of those ordained spend only a short period in the order, typically the four months of the rainy season. In Sri Lanka, fewer take ordination and the expectation is that those who do will remain in the order for life.

Ordination is an option for any male at any age. It, of course, serves as the mode of entrance into the monastic life; but typically it is undertaken between the ages of ten and eighteen. It is then like confirmation or bar mitzvah, a rite of passage from youth to adult responsibility. The ordinand ritually dies and is reborn; he gives up family and friends and all former associations; he leaves off his old clothes, has his head shaved, undergoes a ritual bath, and receives a new name.

Ordination is not an option for women. As we noted in chapter II, the Buddha authorized the formation of an order of nuns. This

A young man being escorted to the monastery by friends and family for ordination. Dressed like a prince and "riding" a friend as his "horse," he follows the example of the Great Renunciation of Siddhartha Gautama.

Thai monks reciting the monastic code (pratimoksha) in the ceremonial hall of the Marble Temple, Bangkok.

order flourished for several centuries, but later declined for unknown reasons. In the mid-fifth century C.E., for want of sufficient nuns to perform the ceremony (a minimum of ten is required), the ordination line lapsed. Women are permitted to take novitiate vows, wear the monastic robe, and live in or near a monastery, but such persons are not considered to be full-fledged nuns and are not given the respect that is given to monks. The few who take this option are usually older women without family. They live in relative seclusion and perform menial tasks for the monks.

Ordination is a communal act. Above all, it brings merit to the community in which it occurs, especially to the parents of the ordinand and those of his ancestors who may be suffering in hell or as hungry ghosts. It is commonly said that the lower ordination benefits primarily the mother, the higher ordination the father. The ordinand is a sacrifice for society. He renounces all worldly pleasures, particularly sexual pleasure, thereby becoming a storehouse of spiritual power for others to draw upon. In some communities, it is believed that the renunciation of sexual activity releases energy or adds to the total fertility potential in the environment, so as to stimulate rainfall. This is one reason for performing ordinations just prior to the rainy season.

In the Mahayana, for example, in the Japanese Zen, monks are usually ordained in the presence of other monks, but the ordination is essentially the act of a **roshi,** "venerable teacher/master," rather than a community of monks. An established, personal relationship between the candidate and a *roshi* is a necessary prerequisite for ordination. The candidate may be ordained immediately upon entering training or only after some months or years of training, depending upon the *roshi*'s perception of his readiness. Ordination is not a puberty rite or a rite of sharing merit with family and the larger lay community. It is a personal commitment and one that is assumed to be for life. The vows of ordination are the same as those for a Theravada monk, with the important exception that the Zen monk does not take a vow of celibacy. Most Zen monks undergo a period of training at a monastery temple and thereafter serve as priests to a local congregation. They marry, live with their family at the temple, and spend most of their time performing rituals for families who belong to the temple. The temples they serve do not have a resident body of monks. Even those monks who, like the *roshi,* stay on in a monastery, may be married.

Ordination to the monastic life is an option for women as well as men in the Mahayana. There has been a continuous tradition of female orders in China, Korea, and Japan since the ordination for women was introduced in China in the fifth century C.E. Nuns are ordained in the same way as monks and commit themselves to the Pratimoksha code as anciently defined. In China, nuns live in seclusion, separate from the monks, and little is known of their way of life. Korean and Japanese nuns function in society in the same way as monks; in Japan, a nun may serve as priest for a community temple.

The monastic practice of Buddhism is ultimately aimed at the attainment of enlightenment for individuals. But in both the Theravada and the Zen traditions, the monk is seen to have an obligation to society. In Sri Lanka, Burma, Thailand, Laos, and Cambodia, the great majority of the people adhere to Theravada Buddhism. Most monasteries are an integral part of local communities. Theravada monks have extensive contact with the laity, in receiving daily food, at ordinations, on Observance days, in receiving new robes during the Kathina festival, in giving blessings at funerals, birthday celebrations, occasions of the start of new business ventures, and public celebrations.

Japanese Buddhism is pluralistic. The relationship between monk and society has a different configuration from that in Theravada countries. Zen monasteries and temples have patrons dispersed among the general population. Monks in training beg for food in the village but rely primarily on their patrons. They perform merit-making rituals by and large only for their patrons. Those monks who serve local temples minister regularly to a group of families residing in the vicinity of the temple.

The way of the laity as practiced in Theravada Buddhism consists of keeping the Five Precepts (to the extent possible in pursuit of the lay life), showing respect for and supporting the monks, spending Observance days at the monastery under the strict **Eight Precepts,** and generally taking every opportunity to gain merit at the hands of the monk. The farmer inevitably takes the life of small insects and animals in tilling the fields and protecting his crop. Lay people take the life of animals for food. Husband and wife necessarily engage in sexual relations to produce children. The demerit of such acts is outweighed by the merit of offering food to the monks and producing a son who becomes ordained as a monk. The lay man or woman may attain the status of a Stream-entrant even in the lay life and someday or in some later life be able to join the Sangha. In the short run, he or she looks to a harmonious and prosperous life and a more favorable rebirth, perhaps in one of the heavens of great enjoyment.

Theravada Buddhism essentially "works" by the mutual dependence of Sangha and lay society. Monks most exemplify the ideal of self-discipline, enlightenment, and nirvana. They are holy persons; their renunciation makes for purity and wisdom; their self-control gives them power over the forces of disease, the destructive forces of nature, and the physical and mental forces that make for pain and stress in human life. At the same time, the monastic life of moral purity and meditation is not possible without gifts of food, clothing, and housing from the laity. These gifts, essential to the material well-being of the monks, are the vehicle by which the laity benefit from the monks' purity and power. The mere presence of the monks is inspiring and auspicious. They are worthy of reverence and gifts. Their reception of gifts conveys merit to the givers. Their ritual chanting of the Buddha's word generates power to heal and protect the laity, to stimulate rain for the crops, and to dispel malicious spirits. The monks' power is a by-product of their striving toward nirvana. The laity provide material support to the monks; the monks exercise their power to bring prosperity to the laity so that they may provide material support. Buddhism is the path to nirvana; it is also the path to the material prosperity that makes the pursuit of nirvana possible.

In the Zen Mahayana, lay Buddhists partake of the merit of the monks through material support of the monastic life and by presence at ceremonies performed by the monks, on the same principle as that functional in Theravada practice, but in a context that places less emphasis upon merit sharing. It is equally important for the Zen laity as well as the monks to meditate. The Mahayana emphasizes that a person's Buddha-nature may be realized in the lay life as well as in the pursuit of monasticism. Zen, in particular, fosters realization in the midst of ordinary life activity.

In the Pure Land Mahayana (Jap., *Jodo* and *Jodo-shin*), there is no monastic Sangha. The way is faith in the power of Amida Buddha who has stored up tremendous merit over the course of eons of time as a *bodhisattva* and who founded the Pure Land. Since Amida has accumulated enough merit for the salvation of the whole world and this merit is available directly to any devotee, there is no need for monks. One has assurance of being admitted to the Pure Land after death by surrender to Amida, expressed by chanting his name with all one's heart. This chant, called the **nembutsu,** is *Namu Amida Butsu,* "Reverence to Amida Buddha." Pure Land Buddhists strive to keep the precepts, earnestly desiring to live a life of compassion, but not as a means of making merit. The pure and compassionate life is to be lived simply in gratitude for what Amida has done.

The Rituals and Festivals of the Buddhist Life

Daily and Periodic Rituals

Merit is made and shared through daily, periodic, and special rituals and yearly festivals. Morning and evening services of chanting or worship take place in every monastery, temple, and home. With the placing of flowers and the lighting of candles and incense before a Buddha-image or some other symbol of the presence of the Buddha, monks chant together and the lay family offers a prayer. The flowers, beautiful one moment and wilted the next, remind the offerers of the impermanence of life; the odor of the incense calls to their mind the sweet scent of moral virtue that emanates from those who are devout; the candleflame symbolizes enlightenment.

The central daily rite of lay Buddhism is the offering of food. Theravada laity make this offering to the monks. Mahayana laity make it to the Buddha as part of the morning or evening worship. In both settings merit is shared.

The weekly Observance Day rituals at the Theravada monastery are opportunities for both laity and monks to quicken faith, discipline, and understanding and make and share merit. On these occasions, twice each month, the monks chant and reaffirm the code of discipline. On all of these days, they administer the eight precepts to the gathered laity—the laity repeating them after the monks—and offer a sermon on the Dharma. The monks pour water to transfer merit to the laity; the laity pour water to share this merit with their ancestors.

Zen monks twice each month gather in the Buddha-hall of their head temple and chant for the welfare of the Japanese people. Pure

A lay devotee offers incense and prayer before a Buddha-image. The Buddha's uplifted hand is in the gesture of "do not fear."

Land Buddhists congregate at the temple once each week to praise Amida.

Rites of Passage

There are special rituals to mark, protect, and bless the occasions of major life transitions. They publicly mark and protect times of passage from one status to another—times of unusual vulnerability such as birth, birthdays, coming of age, marriage, the entering into a new house, and death. Monks preside over ordinations, funerals, and death commemoration rites. In the Theravada tradition, ordination is a puberty or coming-of-age rite; in Zen Mahayana, it does not so function, but nevertheless it marks a major life transition. In the Theravada tradition, monks also preside over birthday and new-house blessing rites. Ex-monks—elders in the lay community—perform the rituals for childbirth and marriage. In Japanese Pure Land, the lay priest presides over rituals of the first presentation of a child at the temple, confirmation of boys and girls at the age of puberty, and death. Japanese Buddhists undertake marriage at the Shinto shrine, presided over by Shinto priests.

Lao monks receiving food offerings on a festival occasion.

Yearly Festivals

Buddhists everywhere celebrate the New Year and the Buddha's birth, enlightenment, and death. The beginning of a new year is, generally, a time for "taking stock" of one's karma, cleansing, and well-wishing. In Theravada communities the New Year is celebrated in mid-April on the lunar calendar and lasts for two or three days. The laity ritually bathe the Buddha-images and sprinkle water on the monks and the elders, showing respect and offering good wishes. The monks chant blessings on the laity, and together they share the merit of the occasion with the dead. The New Year appropriately begins at the end of the dry season and the beginning of new life in nature. The pouring of water is not only an honoring of the Buddha, the monks, the elders, and the dead but also an offering for plentiful rain and prosperity in the days to come. In Thailand, Laos, and Cambodia, the laity build sand mounds (*stupas*) at the monastery or on the bank of the river. Each grain of sand represents a demerit, and placing the grains in the monastery or letting them be washed away by the river symbolizes a cleansing from bad deeds. Bringing sand to the monastery also serves to renew the floor of the compound.

Zen and Pure Land Buddhists celebrate the New Year on the Western calendar. This is an occasion for Zen monks to publicly read large volumes of sacred sutras, thereby sending out cleansing and enlivening sound waves for the benefit of all beings. Pure Land Buddhists hold special services at the temple twice daily in praise of the Buddha Amida.

Theravada Buddhists celebrate the birth, enlightenment, and death of the Buddha on the same day—the full moon of May, called Vaisakha. In Sri Lanka, it is a festival of lights, and houses, gardens, and streets are decorated with lanterns. It is not a major festival in other Theravada countries, but, occurring on an Observance Day, it is at least an occasion for special food offerings to the monks and more than the usual devotion to keeping the moral precepts.

Japanese Buddhists celebrate the Buddha's birth, death, and enlightenment on different days of the year: the birth on April 8, the enlightenment on December 8, and the death on February 15. The birth celebration, Hanamatsuri, is a flower festival and time for ritually bathing images of the Buddha. Enlightenment Day, Bodhi, and Death Day, Nehan (Nirvana), are simply occasions for special worship.

Theravada Buddhists mark the beginning and end of the rain-retreat, which generally coincide with the beginning and end of the rains. They conclude the year with a harvest festival. Theravada monks enter rain-retreat on the full moon of either June or July. The three- or four-month period is a time of relative austerity for both laity and monks. The monks remain in the monastery, spending more than the usual time in study and meditation. No marriages or public entertainments occur in the lay community and the laity are more devout in their attendance of Observance Day ceremonies and in their daily food offerings. The Observance Day on which rain-retreat commences is generally occasion for the entire lay community to offer food and many more than usual undertake to spend the day at the monastery, keeping the monastic precepts.

The full-moon Observance with which the rain-retreat ends is much like that with which it begins, with the exception that the monks gather privately and invite each other to point out infractions of the monastic code during the retreat period. The mood of this Observance is a happy one—the rains have ended (usually), the monks may again move about, and public celebrations are in order.

The month that follows, mid-October to mid-November, is the time for Kathina, the offering of cloth from which the monks prepare new robes. Kathina offerings are typically a group effort—of an entire village, a lay association for merit making, a government agency, or the employees of a prominent commercial establishment. Typically, the group approaches the monastery in gay procession. Upon arrival, the presiding monk administers the Five Precepts to the laity, receives the cloth, and declares the great merit of such offerings. The monks jointly chant a blessing verse and the laity pour water, symbolically transferring a portion of the merit to the ancestors.

Theravada Buddhists honor and transfer merit to their ancestors on every occasion of merit making and sharing. Japanese Buddhists give special honor and merit to their ancestors three times each year: on the spring and autumn equinoxes in March and September and during the month July 15–August 15. The equinox festivals, called Higan, "Other Shore," mark times of transition in nature and therefore are occasions to reflect on the passage of time and the progress of beings toward enlightenment—the "other shore." The period July 15–August 15 is the time when Chinese and Japanese monks used to conclude the rain-retreat. At this time, inspired by the reported act of Maudgalyayana, one of the chief disciples of the Buddha, the monks gather great quantities of food to offer to the ancestral spirits (see p. 133).

In the next chapter, we shall consider the practice of Buddhism in concrete detail and will be able to compare and contrast specific, living examples of the Theravada and the Mahayana. Here let us appreciate that, at the level of ideals, the Theravada and Mahayana are not two distinct systems of Buddhism but choices of "vehicles" within the same system. Indeed, as we saw in Chapter II, this is historically how these traditions functioned in India from their origin to the end of the twelfth century. Both viewpoints are inspired by the Three Treasures—the Buddha, the Dharma, and the Sangha—and both respect these Treasures at two levels: as guides to self-achievement and as merit-power to be shared. If we consider the Mahayana as a whole, represented by Zen on the one hand and Pure Land on the other, we can see that both Theravada and Mahayana offer opportunity for accumulating merit through monastic self-discipline and for dependence upon the merit of others. In the Theravada these two foci are equally emphasized in a relationship of reciprocity. In the Mahayana each is the central emphasis of distinct sects. The Mahayana belief in perfected celestial Buddhas and *bodhisattvas* obviated the necessity of reliance on the imperfect, earthly Sangha and, thus, encouraged the development of devotional lay Buddhism independent of the Sangha. Even so, as we see by the existence of Zen Mahayana, not all Mahayanans turned away from meditation and monasticism.

■

CHAPTER IV

The Dynamics of the
Buddhist Life

We have traced the history of Buddhism from its beginning with a charismatic teacher and his disciples, through its twofold definition as Theravada and Mahayana and its spread throughout Asia, to its emergence as a world religion. By interpreting authoritative texts and generalizing a knowledge of Buddhism as it is articulated and practiced in various parts of the world, we have defined the Theravada and Mahayana as unified systems of belief and practice.

But this generalized Buddhism never existed nor does it exist today as such; it is only a guideline or framework by which we may understand the living Buddhism of a variety of particular cultural settings. As a system of values, itself a product of a particular time and place, spreads to other cultural settings, it is actualized by interplay with the existing beliefs and patterns of behavior, the social system, and the climate and geography of each of these different contexts. The teachings of the Buddha were first offered and received in the context of northeast India c. 500 B.C.E. They were transformed again and again in different times and places in a constantly changing civilization. Carried to other parts of Asia at a particular stage of ongoing development in India, they were again transformed by actualization in the natural and cultural settings of these areas.

Our task now is to give concreteness to Buddhism by considering some examples of Buddhist life in particular settings. We shall consider two Buddhisms of Asia, one Theravada, the other Mahayana, one showing us a total pattern of village life, the other, a distinctive feature in the life of one sect among several functioning in the same environment. These examples, of village Theravada in Thailand and monastery Zen in Japan, should give us a sense of the range of practiced Buddhism as well as the peculiarities of two types. As we have seen in the chapters on history and beliefs and practices, the two foci of practical Buddhism are self-discipline (self-power), on the one hand, and merit sharing (other-power), on the other. Each of the varieties of Buddhism centrally emphasizes one or the other of these foci: in the case of village-Theravada it is the sharing of merit and in the case of monastery-Zen it is self-discipline.

Making and Sharing Merit in Phraan Muan

The Buddhism of the village of Phraan Muan in northeast Thailand is typical of that of villages throughout the country and in many ways of those in neighboring Burma, Laos, and Cambodia. Theravada Buddhism is the established religion of the Kingdom of Thailand. It is a way of life for 95 percent of the country's 50 million people. The Sangha, consisting of approximately 260,000 monks residing in 24,000 monasteries, is nationally organized under a supreme partriarch (Sanskrit, *sangha-raja*) appointed by the king and a council of senior monks and is officially patronized and regulated through The Department of Religious Affairs in the Ministry of Culture. The administrative structure of the Sangha parallels that of the government, and monastic and government officials work hand in hand in matters of national integration and development.

The Village and Monastery

The village of Phraan Muan is situated in northeast Thailand. In 1961 it consisted of 182 families, a total population of 932. The people of Phraan Muan are relatively poor. Their chief occupation, like that of most of the people of Thailand, is rice farming. Because they are without irrigation systems, their prosperity is heavily dependent on timely and adequate rainfall. The houses of Phraan Muan, built on stilts to protect against flood and wild animals, are clustered together so as to permit the greatest use of the surrounding farmland. The village is a tightly knit community; of married couples in the village, 90 percent of the wives and 64 percent of the husbands were born in Phraan Muan and all of the monks of Phraan Muan are kinsmen of the villagers.

The village monastery or *wat* stands apart from the clustered houses, yet it is the hub of village life. Built by the villagers themselves, it consists of living quarters for the monks, a ceremonial hall for rituals pertaining to the monastic discipline, and a preaching hall which serves not only as a place of worship and religious instruction, but also as a primary school and a place for public meetings.

The Inhabitants of Phraan Muan

Just as the world as conceived by classical Buddhism is populated by a variety of beings, so is the world of Phraan Muan villagers. The cast of characters in the life drama of Phraan Muan includes gods and spirits as well as human beings.

The most authoritative and powerful person of the village is the monk of long standing and extensive learning. All monks are revered for their merit and wisdom; the longer their tenure and the more extensive their learning, the more revered. The abbot (head monk) of the Phraan Muan *wat* has been a monk for eight years, six as a novice and two under higher ordination. He has passed all three levels of examinations concerning knowledge of the Thai language, the life and teachings of the Buddha, and the rules of the monastic life. Most of the monks of Phraan Muan at any one time are short-term members of the Sangha; they will have memorized the important chants and sermons and learned how to conduct a basic merit-making rite, but they will not have significant knowledge of the Buddha or the Dharma.

Second to the monks in authority and merit-power are ex-monks who, by the merit of having been monks and by the knowledge of language and ritual texts gained as monks, have become respected elders of the community. There are two ex-abbots among the elders of Phraan Muan.

Also inhabiting and exercising power in the world of Phraan Muan are gods (Thai, *thewada;* Sanskrit, *devata*) and spirits (*phii*). The gods are described as in classical Buddhism, but they are believed to reside permanently in certain of the heavens, rather than being subject to karma, as is so in classical Buddhism. The gods are benevolent toward humans but exercise their power only upon proper invitation. Generally, they are ritually addressed as a category, rather than as individuals. The one notable exception is *Nang Thoranee*, the goddess of the earth, who witnesses merit and mediates in the transfer of merit from the living to the dead. This office is based on her role in the conquest of Mara by the Buddha just prior to his enlightenment.

The *phii* are the spirits of the dead and may be benevolent or malevolent. They are "touchy" but usually malevolent only when their prerogatives are encroached upon. The spirits of humans who died untimely and/or violent deaths, such as women and children who die in childbirth or those who die in an accident, tend to be malicious; they resent the fact that their opportunities for merit were cut off prematurely and/or violently. The most prominent spirits of Phraan Muan are Tapubaan, the "owner/guardian of the village," and Chao Phau, "Respected Father-monk," the guardian of the *wat*. Tapubaan is the spirit of the original owner of the village and dwells in a miniature house at its edge, where the farmland joins the forest. Chao Phau is the spirit of a very devout servant of the *wat*. His presence there is indicated by a statue placed near the Buddha-image. He is also represented as dwelling with Tapubaan in the shrine at the village edge. These guardians look after the interests of the village and *wat* and uphold certain moral values.

When properly honored and fed, Tapubaan exercises his power to bring rain and good crops; Chao Phau, when his permission is sought for ceremonies and festivals at the *wat*, protects and blesses these occasions. Tapubaan punishes those who go to live in another village without his permission and those who cut down trees near his house. Chao Phau inflicts stomachache on those who urinate in the *wat* compound and makes the abbot ill when merit-making rituals are held without his permission. Both spirits discipline those who engage in certain physical labor on the Observance days. Appropriate to their context and function, Tapubaan eats meat, while Chao Phau is a vegetarian. Closely associated with these spirits are other *phii* who guard the rice fields. They are honored regularly with food offerings and are given special attention just before ploughing and after the harvest.

Generally, the spirits of kin who died natural deaths are not bothersome to humans. Those of kin who died violently and untimely deaths and those unknown, neglected spirits who may dwell in trees along the roadside or on mountain tops inflict illness on humans by attacking them or by possessing them.

The Monks of Phraan Muan: Their Life and Services

The monks of Phraan Muan are native to the village. It is a Thai ideal that every young man spend some time as a monk, not with the hope of attaining enlightenment, but to bring merit to his parents and community and to mature in preparation for marriage and adult responsibility. Fifty years ago, it was typical for a boy to spend his daytime hours at the *wat*, serving the monks and receiving his basic education under the tutelage of monks. At the age of twelve or thirteen, he would receive the novitiate ordination and remain a monk until receiving the higher ordination at the age of twenty. One of the elders of Phraan Muan village had followed this pattern, serving as a temple boy for two years, ages ten to twelve, receiving novitiate ordination at age eighteen, and the higher ordination at age twenty. He remained a monk to age twenty-seven, serving as abbot of the *wat* for the last three years. Today it is more usual that, without prior experience of monastery life, a young man will receive the novitiate and higher ordination successively at the age of twenty, just prior to marriage. Countrywide, upwards of 75 percent of the eligible males undergo ordination, but less than 40 percent of those remain monks for life. The great majority stay in the order for only one to three rain-retreats. There is no stigma attached to giving up the vows, even after only a few weeks. It is also acceptable to leave the order for a time and return again later.

In Phraan Muan, there is a very high turnover rate in Sangha membership. At any one time during the 1961–1966 period, there were as few as two monks and as many as fifteen. From 1961 to 1964 a total of twenty-six young men, ages twelve to twenty-four, received either the novitiate or higher ordination; most remained for only a short period. In 1966, there were eleven monks in rain-retreat, nine of whom had been ordained just prior to the retreat. Continuity is provided by two or three long-termers, such as the present abbot, who at the age of twenty-two has been a monk for eight years. Of the 182 families in the village, more than half of their male heads have spent some time as novices or fully ordained monks. Two of them are ex-abbots.

Daily Routine

The monks of Phraan Muan rise at 4:30 A.M., chant together in the ceremonial hall, clean their rooms, and then go into the village to receive their morning food. They move about without design, quietly receiving food wherever it is offered. Only women present food to the monks and they must do so quietly and with reserve. After consuming the food upon return to the *wat*, the monks engage in study and the learning of sutras, which they must chant in various ritual performances. Lunch is at eleven o'clock and is brought to the *wat* by women of the village. This food must be finished before noon according to monastic rule. Before and after lunch the monks take care of personal matters such as washing clothes and bathing and cleaning up the food dishes. Some may nap in the afternoon. Evening chanting takes place in the ceremonial hall at 6:00 P.M., after which there is again a period of study before retiring for the night, around 9:00 P.M.

On the Observance days or "moon days" (Thai, *wan phra*), four times each month, the monks do not go out for their morning food. Women of the village bring food to the *wat* both early and late morning. Novices must sweep the public hall, light the candles, and spread mats in preparation for the chanting of the *Pratimoksha* code. The villagers of Phraan Muan frequent the Observance Day rites only during the rain-retreat months. Some, especially elderly women, will commit themselves temporarily to the monastic precepts and remain at the *wat* throughout the day. The monks may preach to the gathered laity before breakfast and in the evening.

Home Rituals

The Phraan Muan monks are frequently invited to individual homes of the village to perform a merit-making ritual. The occasion may be a birthday or a death anniversary. Less frequently, they are invited to bless a new house, to chant for the cure of illness or the granting of long life, or to bring blessing to those on their death bed.

Thai monks chanting the words of the Buddha in a home-blessing ceremony. The string held by the monks and wound around the silver bowl (right foreground) is connected to the Buddha-image of the domestic altar and passes around the house and the laity who are gathered for the blessing. The water in the silver vessel becomes "charged" or "holy" water during the ceremony and is the means of conveying merit to the dead and to the gathered laity.

The form of these rituals is basically the same. A string, which will act as a "hot-line," is stretched out around the house; it is attached to the domestic Buddha-image, passed through the hands of the abbot or chief officiating monk, wound around a bowl of water, and finally passed through the hands of other monks. The laity sit within the area marked off by the string. The monks then chant the *paritta* called "The Auspiciousness Sutra" (*Mangala Sutra*), during which the abbot drops wax from a burning candle into the bowl of water. As the chant ends, he immerses the candle in the water, extinguishing the flame. The sutra speaks of the great merit of the Buddha, the Dharma, and the Sangha. This merit is symbolically infused into the water. The extinguishing of the candle suggests the power of extinguishing all desire. After this chanting, the monks are fed as sumptuously as possible. Having eaten, they chant the "Victory Blessing" *paritta* and the "Received-with-Satisfaction Blessing" *paritta* and conclude by sprinkling the charged water on the householders and/or around the house as may suit the occasion. In chanting for the cure of illness, a portion of the "hot-line" string is tied around the wrist of the patient to seal in the power radiated by the ceremony.

The "Victory Blessing" *paritta* lauds eight victories of the Buddha over malevolent forces. After each verse of praise, it commends or transfers the power of the Buddha to those who hear the sutra. For example:

> The Buddha, through his ten Perfections, beginning with charity, has conquered Mara the Evil One who, having created a thousand hands all armed, came riding on his war elephant Girimekhala, together with his army. By this power, may you be endowed with conquests and blessings.
>
> . . .
>
> The Buddha, through the exercise of his psychic power, has conquered the formidable robber Angulimala who, brandishing a sword, had covered a distance of three Yojana in pursuit of Him. By this power, may you be endowed with conquests and blessings.[51]

The "Received-with-Satisfaction Blessing" is a chant by which the monks transfer merit as an expression of gratitude for food. A portion of the chant is as follows:

> May all evils vanish, may all diseases disappear, may danger not come to you. May you have happiness and old age.[52]

After the monks have blessed the householders, the latter in turn pour water onto the floor, transferring a portion of the merit to the dead, the gods, and to all beings.

Rites of Passage

The important times of transition and change of status in life—birth, puberty, marriage, and death—are times of great vulnerability. At these times there is need for blessing and protection for the affected parties and recognition of these changes by the community. In Phraan Muan, the monks officiate at ordinations (the puberty or youth-to-adult passage rite for males) and funerals. Former monks, respected elders of the community called *paahm* (Sanskrit, *brahmana*), officiate at pregnancy and childbirth rites and marriages. (This title is a carryover from a time when Brahmanism and Buddhism shared authority in the life of the Thai people.)

ORDINATION

Entering upon monastic life is a stage in the pilgrimage toward nirvana. In the Theravada practice of Buddhism, its immediate importance is as a rite of passage for young men. The preferred time of year for ordination is June or early July, immediately prior to the rain-retreat. Since the rain-retreat is a time of relative seclusion and intense study, it is an ideal time for the new novice to be properly instructed and encouraged. In addition, ordination at this time is associated with a rocket-firing festival, the Bunbanfai, "Merit of (Firing) Rockets," the purpose of which is to stimulate rainfall. The merit of ordination is shared with the guardian spirit-forces who control the rains.

It is customary for candidates for first-time ordination to spend the week prior to ordination at the *wat*, learning the words to be vocalized in the ceremony and "getting a feel" for the monastery environment. The candidate is called a *nag*, or "snake," to signify his potency and to commemorate an occasion in the time of the Buddha when a snake gained admission to the Sangha by magically assuming human form. When the Buddha discovered the snake, he forbade it from the monastic life but promised that it would be remembered on every future occasion of ordination.

The parents of the *nag* consult an astrologer to set an auspicious time for the ordination ceremony. During the morning of the day before ordination, assisted by relatives and friends who wish to enjoy some of the merit of the occasion, the parents gather together the eight requisites for their son's life as a monk: two robes, an umbrella, a food bowl, slippers, a lamp, a razor, and a spittoon. They also prepare food and gifts for the monks. A girlfriend of the *nag*, who perhaps will eventually become his wife, may provide a pillow for his sojourn at the *wat*.

While family and friends make ready, the *nag* goes to the *wat* where the abbot shaves off his hair and eyebrows. Body hair is considered dead matter; its removal signifies the renunciation of the old life. It signifies, specifically, renunciation of concern with personal appearance and sexuality. Thereafter, the candidate returns home to don a red or green loincloth and a fine white shawl. This clothing identifies him with Prince Siddhartha prior to his renunciation. The white shawl also signifies the *nag*'s entrance upon a liminal or neutral state, in transition between his former life and the one to come.

CALLING THE VITAL FORCES

On the afternoon of the same day, the *nag*, his relatives, and friends, particularly the elders of the community, gather at the public hall of the monastery for a *sukhwan* ceremony. This ritual strengthens the young man for his ordeal of entering upon the monastic life by "calling (his) life-forces" (*sukhwan*) together and symbolically sealing them in his body. The ceremony is performed by a former monk who is a respected elder of the community.

The *sukhwan* or "calling the vital forces" ceremony is included in all rites of passage except the funeral. It is the essential element of pregnancy and childbirth rites and in the marriage ceremony. It is also performed for the monks when they enter retreat and for any villager before and after a trip, or military service, and during illness.

The ceremony begins with invocation of the gods and recognition of the power of the Buddha:

> Reverence to the Blessed One, the Holy One, the Perfectly Enlightened One!

The gods are invited to attend the *sukhwan* and give blessing to the occasion—they are, in a sense, channels for the flow of Buddha-power. A central element of the ceremony is a tiered, conical structure built up on a tray and bearing a boiled egg, bananas, flowers, and a lump of rice. The purpose of this centerpiece is to attract the *khwan* (life-forces). Near the cone are placed the eight requisites of the monk's life (robes, food bowl, etc.). A candle the length of the circumference of the *nag*'s head is attached to the cone. It is believed that a person has thirty-two *khwan* or vital forces, the most important of which is that of the head. These forces tend to wander out of the body in search of enjoyment and, therefore, must be called together to ensure a safe, healthy, and powerful transition from one status to another. The head-candle signifies the *khwan* of the head and when lit marks the living presence of this *khwan*.

Another candle, the length of the *nag*'s body from shoulder to waist is attached to the eight requisites. It signifies that the *nag*'s body is to become committed to these articles through ordination. The *nag* sits on one side of the cone and requisites, the elder officiant on the other. They are united by a string, called "the thread of good fortune," which is attached to the cone, then passed through the hands of the *nag* and to the officiant. The officiant lights the candles and then reads a standard text that reminds the *nag* that his mother sacrificed and cared for him as a child and that now it is appropriate that he bring merit to her through his ordination. Next, the officiant calls the *khwan* into the food offerings and candles. He then prepares "holy" water by adding liquor or perfume to the water in a small bowl and sprinkles the *nag*. Placing rice, banana, and egg from the cone into the *nag*'s hands, he transfers the *khwan* to the *nag* and then binds it in the body by tying a piece of white thread around the *nag*'s wrist. Parents and other elders of the community then also tie strings. The ceremony concludes with a blessing upon the *nag* chanted by the monks. They chant the *Mangala Sutra*, the Buddha's words invoking prosperity.

On the morning of ordination day, parents and other villagers take food to the monks at the monastery and then, at the sound of a drum, assemble for the procession of the *nag* to the monastery. The *nag*, the monk who will officiate at the ordination, and the two monks who will act as the *nag*'s companion and teacher are carried on palanquins at the head of the procession. The parents and others of the community follow, bearing the *nag*'s requisites and gifts for the monks. The procession circles the public hall three times—one for each of the Three Jewels—and then proceeds to the ceremonial hall, where the monks await. Before the *nag* is carried into the hall, parents and relatives wash his feet with perfumed water, symbolically removing the last taint of his old life.

The ordination plays out the Great Renunciation of Gautama, the Buddha. The *nag*'s peers act the part of Mara's army and playfully attempt to waylay his progress to the ceremonial hall. Before entering the hall, the *nag* throws a handful of coins to the crowd as a final gesure of renunciation of worldly goods.

Valid ordination requires the presence of at least five monks of higher ordination. At times when sufficient monks are not available in Phraan Muan, others are invited from nearby villages and towns. A former abbot of Phraan Muan is now serving at the district level and frequently returns to the village to officiate at ordinations.

The ordaining monks are gathered on a platform at one end of the hall. The parents stand behind the *nag* with his requisites, the father holding his robes. The *nag* prostrates himself before his father and requests his robes. Giving him the robes, the father then leads the *nag* before the head monk. The *nag* bows before the monk three times, each time reciting the Threefold Refuge and requesting permission to be ordained. The officiating monk takes the *nag*'s hand, instructs him as to the meaning of the Three Jewels, and recites a sutra on the impermanence of the body. The officiant then calls upon the *nag*'s companion and teacher to assist him (the *nag*) in putting on the robes and to administer the Ten Precepts, which the *nag* repeats after them. The parents then present the *nag*'s food bowl and the gifts they have brought for the monks. The officiant places the bowl's carrying-sling on the *nag*'s shoulder and concludes the noviate ordination by giving the *nag* a new name—the one by which he will be known as long as he is a monk.

Those *nags* who are twenty years of age or more at the time of first taking ordination will receive the higher ordination on the same occasion. This involves the *nag* properly answering a series of questions about his health and status. Thereafter the officiant requests that the gathered monks duly admit the novice to full ordination. Their silence indicates assent. The officiant then instructs the new monk concerning his responsibilities, the monks chant the Victory Blessing sutra while the new monk pours water, symbolically transferring merit to his parents and other members of the community, and the parents pour water to transfer a portion of this merit to the souls of their dead parents and other ancestors. The ordination concludes with a feast, first by the monks and afterward by the whole community.

MARRIAGE

In Phraan Muan, the dominant pattern in marriage is one in which the groom comes to live with the bride in the home of the bride's parents. Later, with the marriage of a second daughter or with the coming of children, the first daughter and her husband will move into a separate house in the same compound or initiate a new compound with land given by the daughter's parents. The wedding ceremony is, appropriately, held in the sleeping room of the bride's home. It begins with the arrival of the groom and the performance of a *sukhwan*.

The basic elements in the *sukhwan* rite for marriage are the same as those for the *sukhwan* in ordination. The conical structure of offerings to the *khwan* is preferably made by older married women. Widows and divorced women do not attend since their presence would be inauspicious. The bride and groom and the ex-monk elder (the *paahm*) sit on opposite sides of the ritual cone. Several young men sit with the groom and several young women with the bride, completing a circle with the officiant. The *sukhwan* string passes from the cone through the hands of the women attendants, bride, groom, and men attendants and ends with the officiant. The ceremony begins when the elder places bamboo rings with pieces of cotton fluff attached on the heads of the bride and groom. After lighting a candle, he chants, inviting the gods to come and witness the ceremony and bless the couple. Thereafter, he calls the *khwan* to come from wherever they may be and reenter the bodies of the bride and groom. In reciting this call, he states that the marriage is approved by the parents, the elders, and the gods. Then he instructs the couple as to their proper behavior in marriage, in relation to each other and to the parents on both sides. The elder then prepares "charged" water by adding liquor or perfume to a vessel of water and sprinkles the couple.

Placing a portion of the *khwan* food in the hands of the groom, he transfers the *khwan* to the groom's body and then ties a piece of white string around his wrist. After he has done the same for the bride, first the elders and then the younger persons present add strings to the wrists of the couple and present them with gifts of money. Following the *sukhwan*, there is a brief ceremony in which a bowl containing candles and flowers is offered to the elders by the couple through the elder-officiant, and the latter lectures the couple, at more length than previously, on their behavior toward each other and the elders in marriage. The lecture concluded, an older married woman leads the couple to view their sleeping quarters on the other side of the room. The elder distributes candles and flowers to all those present, thereby marking them as witnesses to the marriage. The parents then provide food for the guests and the new couple.

DEATH RITES

The funeral rite is the most important rite of passage. Soon after death, the immediate relatives of the deceased bathe the body and dress it in new clothes. Then they ritually bathe the corpse by pouring water on the deceased's hands, herewith showing respect for the person and asking his or her forgiveness. The body is laid out face up, the head toward the west; the feet are tied together with a thread; and the hands are placed in a prayerful posture on the chest and tied together. A coin is placed in the mouth and flowers, candles, and paper money in the hands. The money is said to be for buying entry to heaven and the flowers and candles for worshiping the Buddha. The mouth and eyes are then sealed with wax.

The entire village community assists in the funeral arrangements. Women prepare food, cigarettes, and betel nut chews. The men construct a coffin and gather wood for the cremation. Everyone contributes small amounts of money to defray the expenses of the funeral.

The body is placed in the coffin along with several articles used by the deceased, a basket of food, and a vessel of water. It is believed that the deceased will use the personal articles in heaven and the food and water are for his or her spirit. When all is made ready, the monks come to the home, take food, and afterward chant near the body. The intent of the Buddha-words chanted is to call together the elements and spirit of the deceased, which tend to disperse at death, to increase the merit of the deceased, and to show the spirit the way to heaven.

The chanting concluded, the coffin is carried from the home in procession to the cremation ground near the *wat*. Before they lift the coffin, the coffin-bearers are given flowers and candles with which they will later pay respects to the deceased so that his spirit (*phii*) won't attack them. The monks lead the procession, holding a string that is attached to the coffin. This keeps the deceased within their merit-field during the journey. Upon reaching the prepared pile of firewood, the coffin is carried around the pile three times, signifying the hope that the deceased will be reborn as a human being, will have a spouse and children, and will lead a good life. The coffin is placed on the ground, the monks chant, then receive gifts of tobacco, betel nuts, and money, and again chant a blessing in response for the gifts. Monks and relatives "cleanse" and "beautify" the corpse by pouring coconut juice and scented water on the face. Their sentiment in this act is that the deceased may fare well in rebirth. After further chanting, the coffin is placed on the pile of wood and both monks and laity ignite the fire. The monks chant while the body burns.

On the way home, the villagers go first to the *wat* to rid themselves of any bad effects resulting from association with death. On the evening of the day of cremation and again the next two evenings, monks perform a blessing rite at the home of the deceased. They chant holding onto a string attached to a Buddha-image, a bowl of water, and the collected items belonging to the deceased or items used in the funeral proceedings. The effect of these rites is to purify or neutralize the latter objects and again bring merit to the family and friends of the deceased. On the morning of the third day after cremation, a party of monks and villagers collect and wash the bones of the deceased and place them in a pot. The pot is covered with a cloth secured by a string, one end of which is left dangling. The pot is then placed on the "chest" of a human figure fashioned on the ground with the ashes of the funeral pyre. The monks chant first near the pot and then while holding onto the string. This concluded, the cloth covering of the pot is pierced to allow the spirit of the deceased to depart and the pot is buried. It is believed that the spirit is now on its way to heaven. In some parts of Thailand, a portion of the ashes and bones of the deceased are enshrined in the home or in a *stupa* constructed in the *wat* compound.

Following this ceremony, villagers and monks gather at the *wat*, the women present food to the monks, and close relatives make food offerings to the spirit of the departed and offer to the monks a palanquin of gifts that had been prepared by the community the day before. The gifts are items of use to the monks, such as a robe, a flashlight, or a pillow. One of the monks responds with a sermon, the import of which is that life is impermanent and that those who perform funeral rites gain great merit for their deeds.

The Yearly Round of Communal Rites and Festivals

Family merit-making rituals and rites of passage take place at various times, appropriate to the changing circumstances of families and individuals. Certain collective or all-village rites and celebrations take place every year, at the same time each year, and as ways of marking time and focusing power for the whole community. The events of this yearly cycle are determined with reference to the key moments of agricultural endeavor, the great events of the life of the Buddha, and the major points of transition in the life of the Sangha. For the most part, the events of these three patterns are coordinated with each other to make for a harmonization of all of the life resources operative in the village environment.

NEW YEAR

The lunar year begins April 15, which is seasonally at the end of the dry period when the villagers look forward to the rains. It is a time for cleansing, sharing merit with the dead, and invoking rain. The New Year is celebrated on three successive days: the first marks the end of the old year, the second is a day of transition, and the third is the actual New Year's Day. On these days women take food to the *wat* in the early morning as well as the late morning, and each evening the monks chant *parittas* of blessing. The last day of the old year is a time for ritually bathing the Buddha-image and sprinkling water on the monks. By this act the laity cleanse themselves of the bad karma accumulated during the past year and symbolically refresh the Buddha and the Sangha for the year to come. The second day of the celebration is a time for remembering ancestors and transferring merit to them. During the day, the monks chant at the cemetery, some of the laity build and decorate sand *stupas* (Thai, *pagodas*) in the *wat* compound, and young people ritually bathe their elders with perfumed water, asking their forgiveness and blessing. In the evening, monks and laity gather near the sand *stupas* and the monks chant the Victory Blessing *paritta*. New Year's Day is a time for reveling; characteristically the young playfully shower each other with water.

BUDDHA DAY

In May the rains begin and the fields must be plowed and planted. The full-moon day is a time to remember and celebrate the birth, enlightenment, and death of the Buddha. In Phraan Muan, the day is marked by the laity taking food to the monks early in the morning and in the evening processing three times around the ceremonial hall of the *wat* with lighted candles and incense. *Visakha Puja*, as the day is called, is a national holiday in Thailand. Many towns and villages celebrate it more elaborately than the people of Phraan Muan. Usually, for instance, following the candlelight procession, monks and laity gather in the public hall of the *wat* for a lengthy recitation of the life of the Buddha, displaying this life as a paradigm for all life and a paragon of power for the new year.

THE ROCKET FESTIVAL

In mid-July the monks enter the rain-retreat. Leading into the retreat, ordinations are performed and the village holds a rocket-firing festival (*Bunbangfai*, literally, "Merit of [Firing] Rockets"). This is the time of year when the young rice plants are growing and there is need for plentiful rain. The merit-power of ordination and the festival of rockets are addressed to the village guardian deities who are believed responsible for rain. The rocket festival begins the day after ordination day. A number of rockets—as many as the villagers can afford—are constructed at the *wat* with the help of the monks several days prior. Two special rockets, one called "rocket for paying respect" and the other "wishing rocket," are made for honoring Tapubaan, the village guardian spirit.

On the first day of the festival, the rockets are carried in procession to the dwelling of Tapubaan at the edge of the village. The participants have been drinking and there is much boisterous reveling. The procession proceeds from the *wat* and, arriving at the spirit dwelling, circumambulates the dwelling three times. After a prayer by a villager believed to be in special communion with the spirit, in which rain, good health, prosperity, and health for the livestock is requested, the "paying respect" rocket is fired, and the procession returns to the *wat*, circumambulating the public hall three times.

In the evening, the villagers enjoy dancing, folk opera, and the like in the *wat* compound and the monks chant to bless the remaining rockets. The next morning, the monks are feasted at the *wat*, and thereafter monks and laity gather near the rice fields and one after the other fires the rockets. The "wishing rocket" is fired first. If it flies straight and high, it is believed that there will be prosperity. The firing of the other rockets is a time for much "horseplay," for monks and laity alike. Those whose rockets do not fly well are pelted with mud.

ENTERING RAIN-RETREAT

The revelry of the rocket festival is followed by the solemnity of entering upon the rain-retreat. The day is the full moon of July. In the morning, the laity make merit by feeding the monks. Then, the lay elders perform a *sukhwan* ceremony for the monks, calling and binding in their vital forces in preparation for retreat. Following the *sukhwan*, the monks are presented with bathing cloths for use during retreat and the monks respond with a blessing and a short sermon on the merit of the occasion. In the evening, there is a candlelight procession like that of Visakha Puja day and the monks chant a final blessing *paritta*.

HONORING THE DEAD

In the month of September, when the rice is in a critical growing stage, the villagers celebrate *Bun Khaw Saak*, the festival of "making merit with puffed rice." This is a time when the spirits of the dead visit the earth, as they do on the day before New Year. If they and the guardian spirit of the rice crop are fed and offered merit, they will protect the crop. After offering food to the monks and listening to a sermon, the laity place packets of puffed rice and vegetables on the ground near the ceremonial hall of the *wat* while the monks chant and pour water, transferring merit to the dead. At the same time, puffed rice is placed in the paddy fields, so that the rice sprit and the ancestors, coming there for food, will be pleased by the fact that the fields have been well kept. Puffed rice, which is rice that will not grow again, or "dead rice," is the preferred offering to the dead. By contrast, raw rice, which suggests life and fertility, is offered in the marriage ritual.

CONCLUDING RAIN-RETREAT AND KATHIN

On the full moon of October, the monks conclude their retreat. They have been "growing" by discipline and study as the rice has been growing and now emerge from relative seclusion as the rice

grains are coming to maturity. Early in the morning the monks perform the invitation rite in the ceremonial hall, inviting each other to
point out infractions of the discipline during the retreat. Afterward
the laity bring food and gifts to the monks and themselves take a
communal meal at the *wat*. When the meal is finished, the elders
listen to a sermon and the young people frolic, lighting firecrackers
and throwing puffed rice on the Buddha-image. In the evening
there is a candlelight procession.

The end of the rain-retreat is marked in a grand way by the festival of Bun Kathin, "the merit of giving robes," which occurs some-
time between the full moon of October and that of November. The
festival lasts for two days. On the morning of the first day the public
hall of the *wat* is decorated and gifts for the monks are assembled on
a wooden palanquin. It is customary in Thailand that the gifts for
Kathin should be provided by donors from another village; failing
this, they are provided locally. The palanquin is elaborately decorated to look like a palace. It is said to signify the hope for a heavenly
rebirth. Carved serpents on the roof ends represent the Buddha's
conquest of desire, and pin cushions hung from the four corners of
the roof signify the hope for rebirth with sharpness of mind. On the
evening of the first day, a blessing by the monks is followed by dancing and folk opera in the *wat* compound.

The next morning the villagers gather for a procession of the
"palace" of gifts around the public and ceremonial halls. The procession is led by an ex-monk bearing a Buddha-image on his head.
Behind him are monks holding onto a yellow string attached to the
palanquin. Between the monks and the palanquin are men of the
village, bearing money trees—branches on which are hung paper
money and small gifts for the monks. These trees are said to imitate
the great wishing tree that stands in the Tusita heaven and grants all
wishes. Other participants carry flags bearing the image of Nang
Thoranee, the Earth Goddess, and aquatic animals. (According to
Thai legends, the Earth Goddess, when witnessing to the perfection
of the Buddha, wrung a flood of water and aquatic creatures from
her hair, thereby dispersing Mara's army.) After the procession has
entered the public hall, a yellow string is tied around the hall to
mark the boundary within which merit will be received. The ceremony begins with a lay elder requesting one of the monks to administer the Five Precepts to the gathered laity. Then, an elder presents

new robes to the abbot, another presents the money trees, and the ceremony is concluded with a blessing chant.

THE HARVEST FESTIVAL

Appropriately, the climactic merit ritual of the year occurs in February after the harvest. The festival is called Bun Phraawes, "The Merit of the Venerable Wes (Vessantara)." The next to last birth of the Buddha was that as Prince Vessantara, who showed perfection in charity. The recitation of the life story of Vessantara is one of the central acts of the festival. The festival brings together the powers of nature, the gods, and human beings, in order that all may share in the merit of the Buddha.

On the first day of the festival, monks sit, together with a Buddha-image, in a grand pavilion constructed for the occasion and receive gifts of rice paddy. Late in the afternoon, monks and elders lead a procession to a pond near the village, where they invite the serpent (*naga*), lord of the waters, to the *wat* to hear the story of Vessantara. The spirit-lord of the waters is believed to have power over Mara—the power to protect the activities of the festival from Mara's onslaught. He is enticed to the festival with gifts, which include a food bowl, robes, and other requisites of the monk's life, flowers, puffed rice, and cigarettes. After an elder chants the invitation to the spirit, guns are fired and drums are beaten and the monks chant the Victory Blessing. A kettle of water is then taken from the pond; this water is the spirit. Two small Buddha-images are placed in the kettle of water, completing the harnessing of the spirit's power to the Buddha and the blessing of the festival. The kettle is carried in procession back to the *wat* and placed on a high shelf in the public hall, where the story of Vessantara will later be told. In the evening, the monks chant blessings and a fair is held at the *wat*. On the afternoon of the next day, the villagers gather for a special sermon concerning a virtuous monk who preached to both the inhabitants of hell and those of the heavens.

Very early the next morning (2:30 A.M.) the villagers gather at the public hall to invite the gods to the festival. Older men and women carrying flowers, candles, and balls of rice process around the hall three times, each time dropping some of these offerings in baskets attached to flagpoles at each corner of the hall. When the procession is concluded, the elders take the baskets, which are now the residence of the gods, into the hall and place them near the pulpit. After the presentation of flowers, candles, and incense before the Buddha-image and the recitation of the Five Precepts, the story sermons begin. The first tells of the Buddha's renunciation, the second tells of his victory over Mara, and the third is the story of Vessantara. The recitation lasts throughout the day.

Making and Sharing Merit

The central feature of life in Phraan Muan is making and sharing merit. Making and sharing are inseparable. Life goes on by exchanges of merit. Young men renounce worldly enjoyments to bring merit to their parents and community. They, of course, earn merit for themselves by their moral discipline and study; but the emphasis in their becoming monks is on service to the community. In turn, they are fed, clothed, and housed by the community. They enjoy the highest respect of anyone in the village and are free from labor in the fields. They have opportunities to travel. They are the beneficiaries of the merit of the laity. The fruits of labor are the merit of the laity. Sharing it, by feeding, clothing, and housing the monks and by bearing the cost of sponsoring ordination and honoring the gods and spirits whose power provides prosperity, they gain greater merit. The ex-monk, by the fact of his previous service and study, has merit second only to that of the monk and enjoys high status in the community. He shares his merit by mediating between the monks and the lay community and by facilitating the times of transition (marriage, childbirth, illness, entering rain-retreat, etc.) in their lives. The living make merit for the dead in reciprocation for the merit that the dead relatives brought to their lives while they were alive. Human beings share their merit to empower the guardian spirits of the village, *wat*, and crops.

The villagers give highest priority to the merit of financing the building of a *wat*. This act is reserved for only the very wealthy. But second priority is given to the merit of becoming a monk or having a son become a monk. Although this is costly due to the fact of the expenses incurred for ordination and the loss of the labor of the one ordained, the entire village joins in sharing the expenses (and therefore the merit) of ordination, and the loss of a field hand is more than compensated for by the services performed by a monk. In order of priority, the merit of contribution to the repair of the *wat*, giving gifts to the monks at Kathin time, giving daily food to the monks, observing moon days, and adherence to the Five Precepts rank below building a *wat* or sponsoring or undergoing ordination. Everyone can participate at some of these levels of merit making and sharing. The preparation and offering of food to the monks is the special province of the village women, repair of the *wat* the province of the men. The elderly, who do less of the field work, are free to observe the moon days; their merit is shared by their family members. Adherence to the precepts, a pillar of the lay life as defined in classical Buddhism, gets a low priority, perhaps because it is just assumed as basic to the Buddhist life and its performance is the least spectacular or publicly displayed. Every communal merit-making ritual begins with the recitation of the precepts under the administration of one of the monks.

The Training of a Zen Monk

Our second example of Buddhism in practice concerns the training of a monk in the Rinzai sect of Zen Buddhism.[53] The Zen tradition in Japanese Buddhism is centrally a tradition of seeking enlightenment through meditation (Jap. *zen*; Sanskrit, *dhyana*). This tradition is preserved and perpetuated by masters who, through years of arduous practice under other masters, have mastered the Dharma and have become recognized as enlightened. The master (*roshi*, literally, "venerable teacher") may be a monk, nun, layman, or laywoman; and indeed the training described below is open to the laity as well as to the monks. Most of the living masters are monks and the spiritual heads of monastery temples, where they guide both lay and monastic disciples in meditation.

The great majority of the monks of the Zen tradition serve as priests in local temples, where their primary function is to perform rituals honoring the dead. They are married, live in the temple with their family, and will be succeeded as temple priests by their sons. Generally, these monk priests do not teach meditation; but they are expected to train under a *roshi* at one of the monastery temples for at least three years. A small number of Zen monks remain in the monasteries, continuing their training and serving the *roshi*. Some of them will themselves become *roshis*.

The large monastery temples of the Rinzai sect offer two training terms per year: the summer or rain term from May through October and the winter or snow term from November through April. During the first three months of each term (May–July and November –January), the monks are expected to remain in the monastery, observing a rigorous discipline. These periods are comparable to the rain-retreat period in Theravada monastic practice. During the second portion of each term the monks may continue their sitting-meditation practice, but they are free to go on pilgrimage, return to their home temple, or engage in such things as gathering vegetables for the monastery in the countryside.

A monk priest learns his temple duties from his priest father. What he must learn at the monastery is self-discipline, humility, and a special kind of awareness. Discipline begins before he departs his home temple. He must dress in a formal robe, cotton leggings, straw sandals, and a large bamboo hat; he must carry food bowls and a small box containing a robe, a razor, books, and enough money for his funeral rites lest he meet with an accident. Ideally, he travels to the monastery, however far, on foot.

The large monastery typically consists of seven buildings of varying size: an entrance or reception hall, a Buddha-hall for formal chanting or prayer services, a Dharma hall for lectures on the sutras, a meditation hall (*zendo*), a latrine, a bathhouse, and a refectory storehouse. These structures are enclosed by a high wall with an imposing gate.

In a typical scenario, arriving at the monastery, the monk traveler passes through the gate, knocks on the door of the entrance hall and, bowing deeply, requests permission to enter for training. Now begins his first lesson in humility and perseverance. He is turned away by a monk at the entrance and told that there is no space available. If he earnestly desires to enter, he remains bowed outside the door, supplicating for admission. The guard then pushes him outside the main gate and firmly shuts the gate. There the traveler sits throughout the day and into the evening. As it begins to grow dark, humbled and tested by his ordeal, he is finally invited in to spend the night in the guestroom of the entrance hall. Inside, he is given a cup of tea and a sleeping mat and is instructed to sit facing the blank wall of the room until bedtime at nine o'clock.

The next morning, he is given breakfast and directed to return outside the gate, to spend the day crouched down in a posture of submission. If he perseveres in this, at evening he is again invited to the guestroom and instructed to meditate, simply sitting crossed-legged, facing the wall. After breakfast each day for five days he must visit the quarters of the administrative head of the monastery and pay his respects, then return to his room for sitting meditation. During this time, he is under surveillance. If he is perceived to be serious in his solitary sitting, he is invited to join the other monks in the meditation hall and thus becomes "a novice in training" (*un-sui*). From then on for the next three months he will spend most of his time in this hall meditating, chanting, and sleeping.

The *zendo* (meditation hall) is a large rectangular hall twice as long as wide, with a door for formal entrance and exit at one end and one for informal entrance and exit at the other. There is a raised platform along each of the long walls, where the monks meditate and sleep. Just inside the formal entrance is the altar of Manjushri, the *bodhisattva* of Wisdom.

The new novice must bow in respect to Manjushri upon entering the hall. Then he is shown to his mat on the platform, a space about four feet wide and seven feet long, where he will spend much of his training time. Behind the mat, on the wall, is a shelf for his meager belongings and his sleeping mat. The rules of conduct during training are posted outside the informal entrance to the *zendo*, but the elder monks, especially the ones who supervise behavior in the hall, take care to instruct the novice as activity proceeds.

In a few days, the novice is summoned to his first meeting with the *roshi*. He must prostrate himself three times at the entryway to the master's quarters and, upon entering, present incense sticks or incense money to show his submission to training under this master. The two have tea and the master kindly enquires about the welfare of the novice, his name, and hometown. Future meetings with the master, part of the training, will not be so cordial, as it is the master's task to awaken the novice to his Buddha-nature and this will require severe questioning and harsh treatment.

The Daily Routine

The monks are awakened at 3:30 A.M. by the tinkle of a small bell. They use the toilet and wash face and hands with a few cups of water. Although there is plenty of water available, they are admonished to conserve. At the sound of a gong, they adjust their robes and walk quickly and quietly to the Buddha-hall for the morning service. Entering the hall, each monk bows before images of the Buddha and certain of the great masters such as Bodhidharma and Eisai that adorn the altar. Then follow thirty minutes of chanting from the sutras from memory. Monks who are slow waking up are encouraged by a slap with a stick, administered by an elder monk. The service ends with the chanting of the four vows of the *bodhisattva*:

> However innumerable beings are, I vow to save them;
>
> However inexhaustible the passions are, I vow to extinguish them;
>
> However immeasurable the Dharmas are, I vow to master them;
>
> However incomparable the Buddha-truth is, I vow to attain it.

A Zen monk engaged in a tea ceremony.

A similar evening service of chanting takes place in the Buddha-hall late in the afternoon.

After the morning service, the main body of monks returns to the *zendo* for chanting of reverence to Manjushri, followed by a cup of tea. This is not a "tea break." The tea is served and drunk in a very meticulous manner as part of a total program of cultivating heightened awareness. The chanting for Manjushri, the *bodhisattva* of Wisdom, "awakens" and "enlivens" this patron of the meditation hall and, most of all, creates an appropriate mind-set among the monks for their daily striving after wisdom. While this is taking place, the monks who have been appointed to administrative duties for the term are chanting to the guardian spirit of the monastery, who is enshrined in the monastery office. The monks attribute a living spirit to the monastery, which is indicative of a deep humility and respect toward nature. The emphasis in honoring Buddha, *bodhisattvas*, former masters, and spirits is on the state of mind created thereby, not on the objective existence of such beings.

Breakfast follows the morning services. The monks eat three meals a day; early morning, at ten o'clock, and in the evening. Breakfast is a small quantity of rice, pickled plums, and vegetables; lunch is a heavier meal, consisting of rice mixed with wheat, soup, vegetables, and pickles. Since it is recognized that the evening meal is contrary to the rules of the ancient Indian monastic code, this meal is simply leftovers from the midday meal and is called "medicinal food."

All food is prepared by monks in the monastery kitchen. The monks do go into the town to receive donations eight times a month—on the first, third, sixth, eighth, eleventh, thirteenth, sixteenth, and eighteenth days—but the donations are raw rice and money rather than cooked food. The monks walk the town for about three hours in sets of three, their eyes shielded by their large bamboo hats. As they walk, they chant over and over, "Ho . . . u," "rain of Dharma." They receive the donations in a bowl without seeing the donor and respond with a bow and a short recitation. In addition to these begging rounds, which convey merit to the laity in general, once a month monks walk to the homes of lay patrons of the monastery to receive more sizable donations of rice. At the end of October each year the monks gather nonmarketable radishes from the farms surrounding the monastery. All of this food is supplemented by a harvest within the monastery itself. As an important part of their total discipline, Zen monks work a monastery garden. Pai-zhang (Pai-chang), an eighth-century Chinese master, introduced the rule: "A day of no work is a day of no eating."

The monks eat at the refectory, sitting on the floor at low benches. The food is served ceremoniously by the monk on duty, each course beginning at the signal of the head monk. Before eating, the monks chant *The Sutra of the Heart of the Perfection of Wisdom* (*Prajnaparamita-hridaya Sutra*), which gives the essence of the teaching on emptiness (*shunyata*). It begins:

> When the *bodhisattva* Avalokiteshvara was engaged in the practice of the deep Perfection of Wisdom, he perceived that there are the five aggregates; and these he saw in their self-nature to be empty. . . . Form is emptiness, emptiness is form . . . . The same can be said of sensation, perception, volition, and consciousness.[54]

Following this sutra, they invoke ten Buddhas and *bodhisattvas*: Vairocana, Shakyamuni, Maitreya, Manjushri, Avalokiteshvara, and others. At breakfast, there is a verse accompanying the rice gruel:

> The gruel-meal has ten advantages
> Whereby the yogins are benefitted;
> The results accruing from it are boundless,
> Finally leading them to eternal happiness.[55]

At lunch, the sutra and Buddha-invocation are followeed by a fivefold vow:

> Let us think on how much we have accomplished and how this food has come to us.
> Let us accept this prepared food only because we have now performed good deeds.
> Let us take only enough food to satisfy our needs, leaving our hunger not quite satisfied.
> Let us partake of this food as medicine in order to aid our thin bodies.
> Let us accept this food so that we may establish our way.[56]

Eating begins with a verse to the first three morsels:

> The first morsel is to destroy all evils,
> The second morsel is to practice all good deeds,
> The third morsel is to save all sentient beings—
> May we all attain the path of Buddhahood.[57]

The food is taken thereafter in silence and with care not to make biting or chewing sounds. When the meals are finished, short verses are again chanted recognizing that the body is strengthened as an instrument of realizing enlightenment. The monk on duty carefully cleans up any particles of food left on the bench. Outside the eating hall, he first offers these particles to the hungry ghosts and then sets them out for the birds.

After breakfast there is a tea ceremony in the meditation hall. Periodically, tea is taken with the master, who then delivers an address exhorting the trainees to study and work hard in all that they do. Hanging outside the *zendo* entranceway, there is a wooden board that is struck three times daily to mark dawn, evening, and bedtime. The sentiment of the master's exhortation is hereon capsulized in verse:

> Matter of life and death is great.
> Time runs quickly; nothing remains;
> It waits for no man.
> You should not waste your time.[58]

Every morning following tea, each trainee must meet individually with the *roshi*. In accord with what he senses to be the disciple's state of mind, the *roshi* gives the disciple a *koan* (literally, "a public case or legal precedent"), one of several hundred problem-sayings formulated by Zen masters over the centuries. The problem appears nonsensical and usually consists of a statement such as, "Listen to the sound of one hand clapping" or a question and answer:

Q: Has a dog the Buddha-nature?

A: Mu! ("Nothing," "none")

The *koan* is to be reflected on at all times—in sitting meditation, at work, and at night before sleep. It is meant to break open the mind, to cause a disjunction in the ordinary way of thinking and sensing, and thus to occasion a moment of egoless clarity or immediacy with life (*satori* or *kensho*, "seeing into one's own nature," "seeing things as they really are"). Each successive time that the disciple has a consultation with the master, he must show by word or deed his progress in "solving" the *koan*. The master may be harsh, shouting at the disciple or striking him with his hand or a stick. He strongly rejects the disciple until a breakthrough has occurred. Having solved one *koan*, the master gives the disciple another and another.

Every day there are periods of sitting meditation and work in the garden. On certain days each month (as above), the monks must make the food collection rounds. Every fifth day of the month—the fourth, ninth, and so on—is a cleaning day. The monks shave each others' heads; bathe, assisted by others; and clean the monastery halls and sweep the compound. These activities are occasions for selfless service and the cultivation of humility. Menial tasks are frequently found to provide unexpected moments of clarity. The bathhouse and latrine each have a guardian spirit, enshrined therein, who is given special respect on cleaning days. The fourteenth and last days of the month are days of rest. The monks are permitted to sleep late, to enjoy wrestling or simply lounging about, and to partake of special food at lunchtime.

Sharing Merit

Frequently on food-collecting days, monks are invited to take a meal in the homes of lay patrons. These occasions are understood to bring merit to the patrons and their ancestors. Unlike the Theravada practice, where food offerings pass only from the laity to the monk, several times each year the Zen monks prepare and serve food to their patrons at the monastery. On the first and fifteenth day of every month, the monks visit the head temple of the sect and there chant in the Buddha-hall for the welfare of the nation. These dates are consistent with those on which Theravada monks chant the *Pratimoksha* or code of monastic discipline.

Sesshin

One week each month during the retreat portion of the term, the monks engage daylong in sitting and walking meditation (*zazen* and *kinhin*), punctuated by discourses (*teisho*) by the master and individual and group consultations with the master (*dokusan* and *sosan*). This special training week is called *sesshin* (literally, "to collect thoughts"). During *sesshin* the monks take their meals in the meditation hall. They leave the hall only for consultations with the master, the master's discourses in the Dharma hall, and to go to the latrine. The laity are also welcome at these *sesshins*, as long as they are willing to follow the same rules as the monks.

Sitting meditation (*zazen*) is performed in forty-five minute segments, the time of the burning of an incense stick. It is begun and ended by the tinkle of a bell or the clap of woodblocks. There are fifteen-minute intervals between sittings. The practice is akin to the mindfulness meditation practiced in the Theravada tradition, but in *zazen* it is simply sitting in a correct posture and intensely holding the *koan* before the mind. The posture of the body is described by an early master as follows:

> When one wishes to begin *zazen*, he places a thick cushion in a quiet place, wears his robe and belt loosely, and puts all things about him in good order. Then he sits with his legs crossed in the lotus position. First, one places the right foot over the left thigh, then the left foot over the right thigh; or, one may sit in a half-crossed sitting position, in which only the left foot rests upon the right thigh. Secondly, one places the right hand on the left foot, palm facing upward; then the left hand on the right palm so that the faces of the thumbs push against each other. Then, gradually, one raises the body, moving it backwards and forwards, to the left and to the right, to secure a balanced sitting posture for the body . . . . Keep ears and shoulders, nose and naval parallel to one another. The tongue should touch the upper jaw while both the lips and teeth are kept closed; the eyes should remain slightly open so that one avoids falling asleep . . . . Once the physical posture has been well-ordered, one should regulate the breath by pushing forward the abdomen.[59]

The sitting progresses in complete silence and ideally without any breaking of posture. A senior monk walks along the rows of meditators carrying "the encouraging stick" (*keisaku*), which he applies to the shoulders of those who are experiencing sleepiness or muscle soreness. He administers three whacks to each shoulder with the flat

*Zen monk receiving a blow
with "the encouraging stick"
(*keisaku*) during meditation.*

side of the stick. This is usually done by the request of the meditator
and with compassion. The monks bow to each other before the stick
is applied.

Four times each day there is opportunity for individual consultation (*dokusan*) with the master. This is voluntary but strongly encouraged, especially for beginners. The consultation is for encouragement, but often the master is rather harsh if no progress is
notable and those who have not experienced what they consider an
insight are hesitant to approach him. There are times of high ten-
sion, when senior monks physically force a junior to approach the
master and receive his rebuke. Periodically, the master enters the
zendo for an inspection and thereafter holds a group consultation
(*sosan*). Each monk, in order of his time under the master, must
approach and receive comment in the presence of the other monks.

Every three hours the monks shift from sitting to a short period
of walking meditation (*kinhin*). They walk slowly with the hands
on the top of each other held tightly at the chest and their minds still
working with the *koan*. Walking serves the purpose of stimulating
the body as well as continuing the meditation.

Now and then during the *sesshin*, the *roshi* will give a discourse
on a text (*teisho*) to show its inner meaning. At the sound of the
Dharma drum, the monks gather at the Dharma hall. After they are

seated, the master enters with his attendants and offers incense to the founder of the monastery and to his own master (if he is no longer living). With each offering he prostrates himself three times, while the monks chant adoration to the *bodhisattva* Avalokiteshvara (Jap., *Kannon Bosatsu*) and recite the admonitions of one of the great past masters. When these preliminaries are concluded, the *roshi* seats himself in a high chair facing the Buddha-altar and reads a text. He then comments on the text with reference to his own experience. At the end of the discourse, the monks recite the "Four Great Vows" of the *bodhisattva* (as above).

In December, for one week prior to the Buddha's enlightenment day—celebrated in Japan on December 8—an especially rigorous *sesshin* is held in the Zen monastery. The monks sleep only for an hour or two each night and in a sitting posture. It is considered particularly auspicious to attain insight (*kensho*) during this period.

Each three-month retreat period ends with the examination of each trainee in the quarters of the master. If the disciple is hoping to return for the next term, the *roshi* reviews his conduct thoroughly. In some cases, entrance to the next term is denied and this is effectively the end of the monk's training. No other monastery is likely to accept him once he has been turned away.

Periodic Observances and Celebrations

The monks change their robes twice a year, on July 1 and October 15. There is no particular ceremony associated with this act, such as the Kathin festival of the Theravada tradition. October 5 is also memorial day for Bodhidharma (Jap., *Daruma*), the great master who, according to tradition, brought Zen from India to China in the sixth century C.E. Monks as well as laity purchase Daruma dolls and the monks honor the sage with special chanting at the monastery. During the weeks of the autumn and spring equinoxes (September 20-26 and March 18-24), called Higan, some Zen monks undertake long begging tours to various parts of the country. Many of the great masters consider travel a good stimulant to heightened awareness. On the night of the winter solstice (December 21), monks have a sometimes wild party. Lay patrons bring food and wine to the monastery and there is singing, dancing, and general frivolity. Zen monks do not honor the monastic code prohibiting alcoholic drink.

From July 15 to August 15, Japanese Buddhists celebrate Obon, a festival in which food is offered to the ancestors. The festival is believed to be inspired by an act of Maudgalyayana, the great disciple of the Buddha. According to the *Ullambana* (Jap., *Ura-bon*) *Sutra*, by his special powers Muadgalyayana was able to perceive that his mother was suffering as a hungry ghost. He gathered a large number of monks and together they offered bowls of rice to the mother to relieve her suffering. Zen monks are invited to the homes of their patrons to chant sutras to transfer merit to the family's ancestors. In addition, each day they chant in the Buddha-hall of the monastery and throw water in the air, inviting the spirits of the dead to come for food. On August 15, they offer large quantities of food and scatter rice and water. A tablet marked as dedicated "to all the departed spirits of the triple world" and flags bearing the names of Buddhas, *bodhisattvas*, gods, and demons are set up on the altar of the Buddha-hall, and all these beings are invited to the feast by the chanting of *dharanis* (*parittas*) and a prayer:

> It is desired that all the hungry ghosts inhabiting every corner of the worlds, filling the ten quarters, come to this place and partake of the pure food offered to them. You be filled with it, and when you are fully satisfied, you come here, and see to it that all sentient beings in turn are fed by you. It is also desired that by virtue of this magic food you shall be delivered from the pain you are suffering and be born in the heavens and visit as you will all the Pure Lands in the ten quarters; that you come to cherish the desire for Enlightenment, practice the life of Enlightenment, and in the life to come attain Buddhahood. It is again desired that you protect us days and nights so as to let us attain without hindrances the object of our lives. Whatever merit that is productive of this deed of feeding the hungry ones—let it be dedicated to the universal realization of the Supreme Enlightenment and let every being come speedily to the attainment of Buddhahood. This prayer is offered to all the Buddhas and *bodhisattvas* of the past, present, and future in all the ten quarters, and to Mahaprajnaparamita [The Great Perfection of Wisdom].[60]

At the start of the new year (January 1), Zen monks take three days rest from their normal discipline, but they also create auspicious vibrations for all beings by "reading" the entire corpus of *The*

Sutras of the Perfection of Wisdom (six hundred volumes). They accomplish this over three days by reading the title of each sutra and the first and last few pages and then revolving the volumes several times to the right and left between their hands. This is called *tendoku*, "reading by revolving." The texts are written on a continuous sheet of paper, folded back on itself again and again to make pages. Thus they can be opened like a fan. With several monks at the same time chanting loudly and fanning texts back and forth in front of them, it is an impressive performance.

Japanese and Thai Monasticism: A Comparison

We can see a number of similarities and a number of differences between the practice of Buddhism by Zen Mahayana monks and that of the Theravada people of Phraan Muan. Zen monks do not pay formal attention to the ancient monastic code, although while in training they live a highly disciplined style of life. In training, they are celibate, live with a minimum of possessions—more or less the eight requisites—and cultivate a nonviolent reverence for life. As vegetarians, they practice a form of nonviolence that is not a concern of Theravada monks. They do not honor the prohibition against alcoholic drink or that concerning labor in the fields.

Zen monks can probably be said to give more serious attention to meditation than their Theravada counterparts, although most Zen priests do not undergo the rigorous training described above—at least not for very long; and significant numbers of the monks and laymen of Thailand and the other Theravada countries do engage in serious meditation, even if it is not so in Phraan Muan. With or without monastic training, most Zen monks who are temple priests spend most of their life performing rituals for the laity, much as do the monks of Phraan Muan.

Although in training the Zen monks have fashioned a much more self-sufficient way of life than the monks of Phraan Muan, there is still significant dependence upon and interaction with the laity. They continue, in a variant form, the tradition of begging for food; indeed the large monasteries could not exist or survive without reliance on lay giving. The Zen monks' farmwork is more significant as part of a self-discipline than as a way to provide food.

Within worldwide Buddhism, it is unique to Zen that the entire life activity of the monk in training is interpreted as meditation. Rather than separating sitting meditation from other aspects of the monk's life, all activities of the Zen training are conceived of and practiced as meditation—eating meditation, gardening meditation, sweeping meditation, and so forth. This is consistent with the Buddha's ideal of applied mindfulness, but it is not so thoroughly worked out in the Theravada tradition.

Zen monks share merit by the same instrumentalities and with the same understanding of the world of beings as the Theravada monks. Apart from the reference to all beings becoming Buddhas— a teaching peculiar to the Mahayana—the sentiment of the above-quoted prayer for Obon is fully shared by Theravada Buddhists. By the fact of less daily contact with the laity, there are fewer occasions for the Zen monk to share merit. And, of course, consistent with the Mahayana teaching that the way to enlightenment is equally open to laity and monks, there is less concern in Zen with sharing merit among human beings.

CHAPTER V

Conclusion

TRENDS IN TWENTIETH-CENTURY BUDDHISM

We have concentrated on long-established forms of Asian Buddhism. In closing, let us note some new developments in Asia and the current shape of Buddhism in America. Generally speaking, the main trend in twentieth-century Buddhism worldwide has been toward a more vigorous lay Buddhism. Buddhism has been revived in India with an essentially lay emphasis. Theravada monastic and lay leaders of Burma and Thailand have recently come to encourage the lay practice of meditation. In Japan, the laity have founded so-called New Religions. Buddhism in America, although inspired by Asian monks, is essentially a lay Buddhism.

India

Buddhism was revived in India in the late nineteenth century by a Sri Lankan monk, Anagarika Dharmapala, who in 1892 founded the Maha Bodhi Society for the restoration of the Buddhist shrines at Bodh Gaya. Dharmapala's society, headquartered in Calcutta, attracted attention to Buddhism but did not gain many converts. It was mainly an instrument for channeling gifts from around the Buddhist world for the renewal of Bodh Gaya.

According to the 1971 census of India, there were then almost four million Buddhists in India. Most of these were former Hindus belonging to the "untouchable" social classes. Three hundred thousand untouchables were converted to Buddhism in 1956 under the leadership of B. R. Ambedkar (1891–1956). Thereafter, although Ambedkar died within two months of his successful leadership, more than three million other untouchables joined the movement through mass conversions. Ambedkar, himself an untouchable, had managed nonetheless to get a college degree and a scholarship to Columbia University in New York, where he completed a Ph.D. As Minister of Law in the first government of India after independence, he chaired the committee that drafted the Indian constitution. Frustrated in his efforts to significantly change the Indian civil code, he left his government post and began organizing untouchables to cast off their social disabilities as Hindus by conversion to Buddhism. Ambedkar's Buddhism, informed by Theravada teachings and set forth in a book, *The Buddha and His Dhamma* [Dharma], emphasized a rational approach to life and striving for moral order and social equality. He argued that the Buddha and many of his disciples were non-Aryans and that Gautama was essentially a social reformer. The movement is largely a lay movement, although a Burmese Theravada monk initiated Ambedkar and today several Theravada monks are active in the community in teaching roles.

Southeast Asia

Historically, Indian monks were known for their scholarship as much or more than their achievements in meditation. The concern with scholarship was accentuated in Sri Lankan, Southeast Asian, and early Chinese Buddhism, with a corresponding deemphasis on meditation (in the case of Chinese Buddhism, one of the factors that prompted the rise of the Chan (Ch'an) or Meditation sect). Early in the twentieth century, monks of Burma rediscovered and began propagating what they called "the simplified method" of mindfulness training taught by the Buddha. They encouraged lay as well as monastic disciples. Two of the lay disciples of Ledi Sayadaw (Burmese, *sayadaw* = Sanskrit, *maha-thera*, "most venerable elder monk") founded meditation centers. The International Meditation Center at Rangoon, founded in 1952 by U Ba Khin, has come to attract foreigners as well as Burmese Buddhists. Here, lay men and women enroll for intensive, short periods of training, much like the *sesshins* of Zen practice in Japan. The Sasana Yeiktha Center of Rangoon, founded by the monk Mahasi Sayadaw in 1949, has also come into prominence as a center for lay as well as monastic meditation. This center has spawned more than one hundred branches in Burma, Sri Lanka, and Thailand.

An Indonesian monk disciple of Mahasi Sayadaw, Jinarakkhita Thera, was responsible for the revival of Buddhism in Indonesia in the late 1950s. The small but active movement continues to grow, taking inspiration not only from the Theravada but also from the ancient Mahayana (especially Tantrayana) Buddhism that built the great Borobudur *stupa* on the island of Java in the ninth century.

Japan

The most notable of the New Religions or rather, in the case of specifically Buddhist developments, the "re-newing" religious movements of Japan is the Nichiren Shoshu Soka Gakkai, "The Value Creation Society of the Nichiren True Sect." Founded in 1937 by an elementary school principal, Tsunasaburo Makiguchi, Soka Gakkai appeals to the teachings of the thirteenth century monk Nichiren (1222–1282). Nichiren taught that the *Lotus Sutra (The Sutra of the Lotus of the True Dharma)* embodied the only true Buddhism and that simply praising the sutra by chanting its name in faith would result in power and prosperity for worldly life as well as the realization of Buddha-nature. Makiguchi advocated the daily worship of the *Lotus Sutra* by chanting the formula *(daimoku)*, *Nam Myoho Renge Kyo*, "Homage to the Sutra of the Lotus of the True Dharma," before a scroll bearing the name of the sutra *(gohonzon)*. Soka Gakkai came to prominence immediately following World War II, under the leadership of its second president, Josei Toda, and with appeal especially to people of the working classes. In the spirit of Nichiren, who declared all other religions, including other forms of Buddhism, to be false, Toda encouraged aggressive proselytization toward the eventual conversion of the world with a united Nichiren Buddhist Japan as its center. Its membership grew rapidly. Under the leadership of Daisaku Ikeda from 1960, it spawned a political party, the Komeito, "Clean Government Party," in Japan and founded centers in other parts of the world, most successfully in North and South America. Today, Soka Gakkai claims more than sixteen million members in Japan and several hundred thousand in other countries. Its great temple center, Taisekiji, south of Tokyo near Mount Fuji, is the object of pilgrimage by several million devotees each year. Its emphasis on the power of the word of the Buddha is characteristically Buddhist; its aggressive style and heavy emphasis on power for worldly prosperity are innovative.

Buddhism in America

All of the major traditions of Asian Buddhism—Pure Land, Zen, and Nichiren Mahayana, Theravada and Tibetan Tantrayana—have a following in the United States. Indeed, one can find a list of "Buddhist churches" in the yellow pages of the telephone directories of most major cities. It is estimated that there are about five hundred thousand American Buddhists, mostly of non-Asian descent, active in more than three hundred places of worship and meditation.

Pure Land

Pure Land Buddhism was brought to Hawaii and the west coast of the United States by Chinese and Japanese immigrants in the late nineteenth century. Missionaries from Kyoto, Japan, brought the True Pure Land (Jodo Shinshu) Buddhism, founded by the followers of Shinran Shonin (1173–1262), to prominence among the Japanese-American population in the early 1900s. In 1944, the temples of this sect organized as the Buddhist Churches of America with headquarters in San Francisco. This was the beginning of a gradual separation from the head temple in Kyoto. The clergy of the American Pure Land continued to receive their ministerial education in Japan until 1966, when the Institute of Buddhist Studies was established in Berkeley, California. The BCA has a current membership of approximately fifty thousand, consisting mostly of Americans of Japanese descent.

As in Japan, Pure Land in America is a lay movement led by nonmonastic clergy. Unlike the practice of Pure Land in Japan, where worship of Amida is centered in the home and the temple is the locus only for special memorial rites and festivals, American Pure Land worship is centered around weekly (Sunday morning) congregational services at the temple. These services consist chiefly of chanting the *nembutsu*, singing hymns in praise of Amida's power and grace, and listening to a sermon.

ZEN

Zen Buddhism was first brought to note in the United States by the Japanese *roshi* Soyen Shaku, who spoke to the World Parliament of Religions, meeting in Chicago in 1893 in conjunction with the World's Fair. Impressed by the number of Americans who expressed interest in Zen, upon return to Japan, Soyen dispatched several of his disciples to propagate Zen in the United States. Two of these disciples established Zen centers in San Francisco. A third, D.T. Suzuki, went to work for Open Court Publishing Company in Illinois and published numerous books on Zen. Suzuki's writings and lectures paved the way for a number of other Japanese masters to visit the United States, some of whom remained long enough to gather a significant number of disciples and establish strong meditation centers. One of the largest centers today, the San Francisco Zen Center is now under the leadership of an American *roshi* of non-Japanese descent, Reb Anderson. Another American *roshi*, Phillip Kapleau, is leader of the Zen Center in Rochester, New York, which he founded in 1966. There is no accurate count of the number of American Zen centers or their total membership. The centers belong to both the Rinzai and Soto traditions; some of them have branches, but they are not nationally organized. They exist primarily to teach meditation, and for the most part, they do so following the traditional Japanese method and with Japanese language chanting. Some of the centers have farms and mountain monasteries in addition to their city meditation halls. The centers under the leadership of the above mentioned American *roshis* and that of the British *roshi* Jiyu Kennett, a woman who founded Shasta Abbey in California, are beginning to fashion an "American Zen"; for example, they require less rigorous discipline and permit English-language chanting and the use of knives and forks rather than chopsticks.

Nichiren

A chapter of Nichiren Shoshu Soka Gakkai, under the leadership of its third president, Daisaku Ikeda, was established in California in 1960. Initially its appeal was chiefly to Japanese Americans. In the late 1960s, under the Japanese leadership of Masayasu Sadanaga, who changed his name to George M. Williams, the American chapter reorganized independent of the Japanese center, as Nichiren Shoshu of America, and began aggressively seeking converts among Americans generally. Today, there are more than three hundred chapters throughout the United States, with a combined membership of more than three hundred thousand. The focus of Nichiren Shoshu of America is on promoting self-respect and material well-being through recitation of the *daimoku*. The "church" has emotional but no formal ties to the parent society in Japan and its members are encouraged to be patriotic Americans.

Theravada

Theravada Buddhism has not attracted a significant following in the United States. Since 1966, Sri Lankan and Thai monks have been active in the country and have established meditation centers and temples in several U.S. cities; but the number of supporters of these centers is small and consists mostly of recent refugees from Southeast Asia. Nonetheless, the number of Cambodian refugees, most of whom are Theravada Buddhists, is significant and still growing. As they become settled and better organized, the Theravada way will doubtless have greater import in American society.

Tibetan Mahayana

In 1950, the Chinese army occupied Tibet, pursuing a policy in strong opposition to the traditional way of life. Revolt and suppression in 1959 led to the flight of some eighty thousand Tibetans into Nepal and India. A number of these refugees immigrated to Europe and the United States, among them several learned and accomplished Buddhist masters. Two of these masters, Chogyam Trungpa, who died on April 14, 1987, and Tarthang Tulku, have gathered a large number of disciples in the United States and have established several centers for study and meditation. Chogyam Trungpa's largest center is in Boulder, Colorado. One of its branch organizations, the Naropa Institute, has recently become accredited to offer graduate degrees in Buddhist studies. Tarthang Tulku is based in Berkeley, California. Both of these masters have published extensively and have built strong organizations emphasizing study and meditation as cornerstones of the lay life.

The future of Buddhism in America is uncertain. Pure Land

Buddhism appeals mainly to Americans of Japanese descent. Meditation Buddhism—Zen and Tibetan Mahayana—has had appeal to a relatively small number of Americans and chiefly the highly educated. Nichiren Buddhism has attracted a mixed clientele largely of persons who are "down and out" or who feel disenfranchised or alienated from the mainstream of American life. It is clear that the teaching of the Buddha, viewed as a highly rational approach to life, and one or another of several varieties of meditation are appealing to many Americans. The very presence of Buddhist meditation centers and temples and the availability of a large literature on Buddhism have influenced American Christians and Jews to search their own heritage for resources by which to encourage the contemplative life. In the past few years, Christian and Buddhist leaders have initiated a lively dialogue on meditation and prayer. In terms of sheer numbers of adherents—the three hundred and fifty thousand of a total of five hundred thousand Americans involved in Pure Land and Nichiren Buddhism—it is also clear that devotional Buddhism appeals to many Americans. Pure Land and Nichiren have the potential, as shown by their success in Japan, of engaging the working classes.

Concluding Reflections

In its more than twenty-five hundred years Buddhism has become many things to many people. With a few exceptions such as Nichiren Buddhism, it is a notably tolerant, accommodating, inclusive religion. It has assimilated spirit cults in Southeast Asia and Tibet, accommodated to highly sophisticated traditions (Confucianism and Taoism) in China, and established itself as a complement to Shinto in Japan. It has permitted a wide gamut of belief and practice under its banner. Zen and Theravada, although part of two different cultural streams (Chinese-Japanese and Indian) and two different traditions of Buddhism, are not far removed from each other. On the other hand, one may wonder how Pure Land and Zen could be part of the same religion, let alone of the same tradition within that religion.

In general, the inclusivity of Buddhism is rooted in the Buddha's emphasis on practice rather than correct belief, morality rather than formality, and nonviolence. It is rooted in the Buddha's emphasis on subjectively constructed rather than objectively given reality. He considered the merit or demerit of a belief or practical method in terms of psychological function rather than consistency with an objective norm. The teaching that the world is a product of karma places the onus of behavior ultimately on the individual.

The wide variance of belief and practice within Buddhism is permitted by the dual focus of Buddhism from its beginning: on self-power through self-discipline and reliance on other-power through offerings, invocation, and worship. The Buddha "married" these foci in teaching the mutual dependency of monk and society. This marriage remained intact in the Theravada tradition. The bond was loosened in the Mahayana by its advocacy of the career of the *bodhisattva*—a being for others—and therefrom, by its projection of a store of merit into the heavens in the form of celestial Buddhas and *bodhisattvas*. Belief in a store of merit unconditioned by the exigencies of time and space with direct and simple access to all believers, took some of the onus of merit making and sharing off of the monk. And, it permitted the development of lay Buddhisms independent of the Sangha.

Each of the varieties of Buddhism has defined itself by emphasis on one or the other of these foci, in some cases to the exclusion of the other of the two poles. We may consider this in terms of their use of the Three Treasures. Pure Land Buddhism focuses on the Buddha not as a guide but as a savior. Zen focuses on the Dharma as essentially meditation—an instrument of enlightenment. Nichiren appeals to the Dharma as power not as the result of practice but by simple invocation. Theravada Buddhism centers itself on the Sangha.

We began this study with the observation that Buddhism is the pursuit of worldly prosperity, rebirth in heaven, and ultimately nirvana by the making and sharing of merit. Early Western scholars of Buddhism characterized the religion as world denying, essentially pessimistic toward life. Working solely from texts rather than with an awareness of living Buddhism, and even then failing to see the full import of the texts, they generalized from the Buddha's central emphasis on renunciation (monasticism) toward the goal of nirvana. We can see that this is a distortion of Buddhism in theory as well as practice. In both theory and practice and from its very beginning

Buddhism is, in fact, strongly world affirming. Indeed nirvana, the ultimate goal, is the negation of worldly existence conditioned by karma. But worldly existence for Buddhism is the instrument for the achievement of nirvana as well as the context of suffering. Specifically, in the Buddha's path to nirvana, worldly prosperity and the opportunity for rebirth, along with renunciation, are the means; they are the short-range goals and, indeed, the effective functional goals of most Buddhist striving. Social harmony and the accumulation of wealth are strongly and positively motivated by the fact that their existence is indicative of past merit and the foundation for present merit making. For most Buddhists, meditation as well as morality are effectively motivated by the desire for wealth, status, and social harmony. This is inspired by the Buddha's teaching concerning the mutual dependency of monk and society; it is not simply the way Buddhism came to function because nirvana was an abstraction—a too-distant goal—for the average person.

The Mahayana enhanced a positive attitude toward the world with its restatement of the goal as the realization of emptiness, the realization of unity—oneness—through compassion apprehending the world as itself, Buddha-nature. Zen Mahayana, influenced by the naturalism of Daoism (Taoism) as well as this Mahayana interpretation of the Dharma, came to see the mundane world as, in every respect, the arena of meditation. In Zen, enlightenment is easy, egoless flow or harmony with nature; it is here and now and does not look beyond this world. By reason of the Mahayana emphasis on merit-for-others of those who have realized emptiness, Pure Land Buddhists strive in life-affirming works of compassion out of gratitude for Amida's assurance of release from suffering by rebirth in the Blessed Land. Nichiren Buddhists push the nirvana of world negation into the background in unabashed favor of worldy prosperity through the power of the Dharma.

While the great majority of present-day Buddhists follow a devotional path, the distinctiveness of Buddhism among the world's religions lies in its psychoanalytical/meditative approach to the solution of human problems. Indeed, Pure Land and Nichiren Buddhism would make no sense apart from the assumption of the Buddha's conquest of suffering and accumulation of merit by means of meditation. It is significant to the survival of Buddhism through the centuries that meditation and monasticism, the traditional context for the practice of meditation, have always been part of the tradition. Likewise, the current emphasis on lay meditation in Theravada Asia and the popularity of Zen in various parts of the world are important to the survival of Buddhism in the future.

Notes

1. *Majjhima Nikaya* I.247–49, as translated in Edward J. Thomas, *The Life of the Buddha as Legend and History* (London: Routledge & Kegan Paul, 1949), pp. 67–68.

2. *Itivuttaka* 111, as translated in Heinz Bechert and Richard Gombrich, *The World of Buddhism*: (*Buddhist Monks and Nuns in Society and Culture* (New York: Facts on File, 1984), p. 53.

3. *Digha Nikaya* iii.191, *Dialogues of the Buddha,* trans. T.W. and C.A.F. Rhys Davids, vol. 4, *Sacred Books of the Buddhists* (London: Luzac, 1965), P. III, p. 183.

4. *Majjhima Nikaya* 1.37, *The Collection of The Middle Length Sayings*, trans. I.B. Horner, Pali Text Society Translation Series, no. 29 (London: Luzac, 1976, vol. 1, p. 47.

5. *Vinaya Pitaka, Mahavagga* I.11, *Vinaya Texts*, trans. T.W. Rhys Davids and Hermann Oldenberg, vol. 12, *Sacred Books of the East* (London, Clarendon, 1881), P. I, pp. 112–113.

6. *Buddhist Suttas*, trans. T.W. Rhys Davids, vol. 11, *Sacred Books of the East* (Oxford: Clarendon, 1881), pp. 6–7.

7. *Vinaya Pitaka, Mahavagga* I.78, *Vinaya Texts*, pp. 235–236.

8. Ibid., I.6.32, p. 99.

9. Ibid., I.54.3, p. 209.

10. *Buddhist Suttas*, pp. 93–94.

11. Ibid., p. 91.

12. *The Edicts of Asoka*, ed. and trans. N.A. Nikam and Richard McKeon (Chicago: University of Chicago, 1959), p. 58.

13. Ibid., p. 34.

14. D.D. Kosambi, *Ancient India* (New York: , 1965), pp. 176–177.

15. *The Dhammapada* I.1, trans. F. Max Muller, vol. 10, *Sacred Books of the East* (Oxford, Clarendon, 1898), pp. 3–4.

16. *Buddhist Suttas*, pp. 26–27.

17. *Puggala-pannatti* VI.1, *Designation of Human Types*, trans. Bimala Charan Law, Pali Text Society Translation Series, no. 12 (London: Luzac, 1979), p. 97.

18. *Dialogues of the Buddha*, Pt. I, p. 289.

19. Ibid, Pt. III, p. 127.

20. Edward Conze, et al., eds., *Buddhist Texts Through the Ages* (New York: Harper & Row, 1964), p. 105.

21. Henry Clarke Warren, trans., *Buddhism in Translations* (new York: Atheneum, 1984), p. 35.

22. Ibid., p. 44.

23. Ibid, p. 76.

24. Ibid., pp. 76–77.

25. Ibid., p. 81.

26. Thomas, *The Life of the Buddha*, p. 81.

27. *Vinaya Texts*, Pt. I, pp. 86–87.

28. Warren, *Buddhism in Translations*, p. 92.

29. *Buddhist Suttas*, p. 116.

30. *Vinaya Texts*, Pt. I, p. 91.

31. Saddharma-Pundarika or The Lotus of the True Law, trans. H. Kern, vol. 21, *Sacred Books of the East* (Oxford: Clarendon, 1884), pp. 298–302.

32. Ibid., pp. 413–416.

33. *Vinaya Texts*, Pt. 1, p. 95.

34. Nanamoli, Thera, trans., *The Path of Purification* (Columbo: Semage, 1956), p. 256.

35. *Vinaya Texts*, Pt. I, p. 95.

36. Ibid.

37. *Anguttara Nikaya* III.55, trans. F.L. Woodward, *The Book of the Gradual Sayings*, Pali Text Society Translation Series no. 24 (London: Luzac, 1973), p. 79.

38. Nanamoli, *The Path of Purification*, p. 587.

39. *Vinaya Texts*, Pt. I, pp. 95–96.

40. Nanaponika, Thera, *The Heart of Buddhist Meditation* (New York: Weiser, 1971), p. 117.

41. Ibid., p. 118.

42. *Dialogues of the Buddha*, Pt. I, p. 70.

43. Nanaponika, Thera, *The Heart of Buddhist Meditation*, p. 130.

44. Ibid., p. 164.

46. De Bary, William Theodore, ed., *The Buddhist Tradition* (New York: Modern Library, 1969), p. 81–82.

46. Ibid., p. 371.

47. *Vinaya Texts*, Pt. III, p. 75–77.

48. S.J. Tambiah, *Buddhism and the Spirit Cults in North-east Thailand* (Cambridge: Cambridge University Press, 1970), p. 222.

49. *Saddharma-Pundarika*, p. 389.

50. This account is based on S. J. Tambiah, *Buddhism and The Spirit Cults in North-east Thailand*. Tambiah's study of the village of Phraan Muan spans the period 1961–1966.

51. Tambiah, *Buddhism and The Spirit Cults*, p. 216.

52. Ibid., p. 208.

53. This account is based on Daisetz Teitara Suzuki, *The Training of the Zen Buddhist Monk* (New York: University Books, 1965) and Bardwell Smith, ed., *Unsui: A Diary of Zen Monastic Life* (Honolulu: University Press of Hawaii, East-West Center, 1973).

54. Daisetz Teitaro Suzuki, *Manual of Zen Buddhism* (New York: Grove Press, 1960), p. 26.

55. Suzuki, *The Training of the Zen Buddhist Monk*, p. 145.

56. Smith, *Unsui*, no. 28.

57. Suzuki, *The Training of the Zen Buddhist Monk*, p. 146.

58. Smith, *Unsui*, no. 11.

59. Ibid., no. 53.

60. Suzuki, *The Training of the Zen Buddhist Monk*, pp. 81–82.

Glossary

Amitabha Buddha (Chin., [*A-mi-to-fo*]; Jap., *Amida Butsu*). "The Buddha of Endless Light," founder of the Pure Land heaven, which may be reached by faith.

anatman. "No-self," no unchanging soul or self-nature; one of the three characteristics of existence: impermanence, suffering, and no-self.

arhat. "The holy one," one who has conquered all lust, hatred, and delusion; one who has conquered suffering and rebirth by following the Eightfold Path.

Avalokiteshvara (Chin. *Guan-yin* [*Kuan-yin*]; Jap., *Kannon*). "The Lord Who (Kindly) Looks Down," the *bodhisatva* of endless compassion who protects those who call on him in circumstances of great danger or when desirous of childbirth. Originally male, this celestial being is female in Chinese and Japanese Buddhism.

bodhi. "Enlightenment," seeing things as they really are, the full realization of the four noble truths that results in nirvana.

bodhisattva. "A being (striving for) enlightenment"; in the Theravada, the term applies to the Buddha during his many lives preceding enlightenment and to Maitreya, the one who is yet striving and who will appear on earth as a Buddha at some future time. In the Mahayana, the term applies to all those earthly and heavenly beings who are striving toward enlightenment and, most significantly, who are striving for the welfare of other beings, i.e., those who are dedicated to sharing their merit with others.

brahmana. Priest of ancient Aryan religion and later Hinduism, a member of the highest caste; in Buddhist scriptures the term sometimes refers to any morally upright and learned person who is, therefore, worthy of respect and gifts.

Brahmanism. An ancient religion of India, under the leadership of priests (*brahmanas*) who believed that their performance of fire rituals maintained the world and brought prosperity to human life; Hinduism is largely based on Brahmanism.

Buddha. "Awakened one," "enlightened one," the title of the historical founder of Buddhism—Siddhartha Gautama; the Theravada tradition recognizes Gautama Buddha as the one and only Buddha for the present age and as one who has come and gone; the Mahayana recognizes numerous living Buddhas and uses the title "Shakyamuni" (sage of the Shakya tribe) to distinguish Gautama from other Buddhas, such as Amitabha and Vairocana.

Dalai Lama. "Ocean-lama," in the Tibetan tradition a spiritual teacher who is an "ocean" of wisdom and compassion; the spiritual leader of Tibetan Buddhists, once also the ruler of Tibet.

dependent origination. The phrase designating the causal connection between moments arising and decaying in the endless process of life; the formula of dependent origination explains the cause and effect pattern of twelve factors that characterize ego-ridden existence.

dharani. "That which holds (power)," words spoken by a Buddha that, when invoked, have the power to bless and protect the invoker.

Dharma. "That which is firmly established," the doctrine and path taught by the Buddha.

duhkha. "Suffering, unsatisfactoriness, the state of being ill-at-ease," one of the three factors or characteristics of existence (impermanence, suffering, being without self).

Eight Precepts. The moral precepts to be kept by the laity on Observance days; in addition to the Five Precepts (see below): not taking food after noon, not watching or participating in public entertainments, and not adorning the body.

Eightfold path. The middle path between worldliness and asceticism taught by the Buddha; the discipline of morality and meditation by which one gains the wisdom that results in *nirvana*.

Five Precepts. The five moral precepts to be kept by all Buddhists, although with different levels of rigor for the laity than for the monks and nuns: no violence, no sexual misconduct, no stealing, no lying, and no partaking of alcoholic beverages.

Four Noble Truths. The basic and essential teaching of the Buddha: 1) that there is suffering; 2) that suffering is caused by desire; 3) that the cessation of suffering (nirvana) is possible; 4) that the Eightfold Path is the way to the cessation of suffering.

Hinayana. "The little vehicle, the narrow path," the term used by Mahayana (Great Vehicle) Buddhists to designate traditions of Buddhism such as the Theravada, which teach monasticism as the only way to nirvana.

Jainism. A religion of India founded by Mahavira, a contemporary of the Buddha; Mahavira taught that nonviolence and asceticism were ways to overcome suffering and death.

karma. "Action," the consequence or residual energy created by action, particularly, human thoughts, words, and deeds. Karma may be meritorious or demeritorious and causes desirable or undesirable rebirth.

lama. A master or spiritual guide in Tibetan Buddhism, usually, but not always, a monk.

Mahayana. "The great vehicle, the wide path," the Buddhist tradition emphasizing that the way to enlightenment and nirvana is open to all, by means of the merit of Buddhas and *bodhisattvas* as well as monastic discipline.

Maitreya. "The friendly one, the benevolent one," the celestial *bodhisattva* who now resides in a heaven, whence he blesses those who call upon him; he will come to earth as the Buddha of the next age.

Mara. "Death," the name of the personification of desires that lead to repeated suffering and death; Mara was definitively subdued by the Buddha as the latter came to enlightenment beneath the great tree near Gaya.

nembutsu. "Thinking of the Buddha" (Jap.), the formulaic chant or thought—*namu Amida Butsu*—by which Japanese Pure Land Buddhists express devotion to Amida Buddha.

nirvana. "Blowing out (the fires of lust, hatred, and delusion)," the cessation of suffering, freedom from rebirth.

paritta. "Protection (-formula)," words spoken by the Buddha and later by monks that, when invoked, have the power to bless and protect.

prajna. "Wisdom," the wisdom that results from moral and mental discipline and leads to enlightenment and nirvana.

prajna-paramita. "The perfection of wisdom," in the Mahayana, the wisdom sought by *bodhisattvas* and possessed by Buddhas, by which they see all, know all, hear all, and shed compassion on all beings.

Pratimoksha. "Code of unity," the code of rules to be kept by monks and nuns of the higher or full ordination. In Theravada Buddhism, the monks are committed to recite this code in unison on the new and full moons of each month.

Pure Land (Sanskrit, *Sukhavati*; Chin. Jing-tu [Ching-t'u]; Jap., *Jodo*). The paradise established by Amitabha Buddha by reason of his great merit and out of his compassion for suffering beings, who, by faith, may enter his paradise at death.

rain-retreat. The three or four months (June–October) of the rainy season when Theravada monks remain in the monastery and intensify their discipline and study. Lay Theravadins are more devout in giving and more rigorous in attendance of Observance Day rituals during this period.

roshi. "Venerable teacher," (Jap.), a Zen master.

samsara. "Wandering through (lives)," the round of repeated births and deaths caused by karma.

Sangha. "Community"; in ordinary usage, the term designates the order or community of monks following the way of the Buddha.

Shakyamuni. "The sage of the Shakya tribe"; see *Buddha*.

shunya. "Empty, devoid of"; the fleeting phenomenal world is said to be empty—devoid of any substantial, unchanging self-nature. The Mahayana uses the term to emphasize both the lack of self in beings and the lack of substantiality in the natural world. Enlightenment is the realization of the emptiness (*shunyata*) of the self and world.

smriti (Pali, *sati*). "Mindfulness"; the clarity of mind attained through meditation that leads to the cessation of desire and the achievement of *nirvana*.

stupa. A memorial mound or monument, ideally encasing a relic of the Buddha or an *arhat*, and therefore a place where a devotee or meditator may experience the power of the one commemorated by the mound.

sutra. A text embodying the words of the Buddha.

Tathagata. One who has "thus come" or "thus gone" the way of a Buddha; a perfectly enlightened being. This is the way that Gautama referred to himself after his enlightenment.

Tantrayana. "The vehicle of (specialized) ritual," a subdevelopment of the Mahayana in which highly technical rituals are the special means to enlightenment. A *tantra* is a ritual manual and, by extension, the term designates the rituals prescribed in the manual.

Ten precepts. The precepts undertaken by a novice upon ordination to the monastic life; in addition to the eight precepts (see above), a novice vows not to use a high, comfortable bed and not to use money.

Theravada. "The way of the elders," the tradition of Buddhism whose followers believe they are following the original ("elder's way") Buddhism and in which senior monks (*theras*) hold primary authority in matters pertaining to the Buddha's way.

Three Jewels/Treasures. The Buddha, the Dharma, and the Sangha, the three valued resources of Buddhist belief and practice.

Threefold Refuge. The formula recited by Buddhists to affirm their commitment to the Three Treasures.

Tripitaka. "The three baskets," the threefold text embodying the Buddha's teachings and authoritative interpretations of these teachings; the canon of Buddhist sacred writings.

Zen. (Sanskrit, *dhyana*; Chin. *Chan* [*ch'an*]. "Meditation"; the term designates the Japanese meditation sect of Mahayana Buddhism.

The Scriptures of Buddhism

The earliest written accounts of the life and teachings of the Buddha were formulated in both Sanskrit and a dialect of Sanskrit that came to be known as Pali. Monks of the Mahayana tradition used Sanskrit and those of the Theravada tradition used Pali. The Sanskrit version is called *Tripitaka* and the Pali version *Tipitaka*, both terms meaning "The Three Baskets." The baskets, or collections, are called Sutra/Sutta, Vinaya, and Abhidharma/Abhidhamma. The content of the first two baskets in the two versions is very much the same; that of the two third baskets significantly differs, reflecting the differing doctrines of the two traditions. The quotations from "The Three Baskets" in this book are taken from translations of the Theravada *Tipitaka*, which is outlined below.

In addition to the *Tipitaka*, the Theravada tradition recognizes the *Milinda-panha* and the *Visuddhimagga* as authoritative treatises on the Buddha's teachings. The Mahayana recognizes a large number of texts beside the *Tripitaka*, some of which Mahayanans consider of greater importance that the early threefold collection. The more important of these are detailed below.

The Theravada Texts:

Tipitaka ("Three Baskets")
Sutta Pitaka ("Basket of Discourses")

1. Digha-nikaya ("Division of Long Discourses")
2. Majjhima-nikaya ("Division of Middle-length Discourses")
3. Samyutta-nikaya ("Division of Connected Discourses")
4. Anguttara-nikaya ("Division of Gradual Discourses")
5. Khuddaka-nikaya ("Division of Little Discourses")

Vinaya Pitaka ("Basket of Discipline")

1. Sutta-vibhanga ("Division of Rules")—this is the Patimokkha (Sanskrit, *Pratimoksha*)—the Code of Discipline

2. Khandhaka ("Sections")
   a. Mahavagga ("Great Group" of disciplines for the monastic life)
   b. Cullavagga ("Small Group")
3. Parivara ("Summaries")

Abhidhamma Pitaka ("Basket of Higher Teachings")

1. Dhamma-sangani ("Enumeration of Dhammas")
2. Vibhanga ("Divisions")
3. Dhatu-katha ("Discussion of Elements")
4. Puggala-pannati ("Designation of Individuals")
5. Katha-vatthu ("Subjects of Discussion")
6. Yamaka ("The Pairs")
7. Patthana ("Activations")

The entire Tipitaka may be found translated in the two multivolume sets: *Sacred Books of the Buddhists.* (London: Luzac & Co.), and *Pali Text Society Translation Series.* London: Luzac & Co.

Selections from the Tipitaka may be found in H. C. Warren, *Buddhism in Translations*, Harvard Oriental Series, vol. 3 (Cambridge, Mass.: Harvard University Press, 1922); *Milindapanha* ("Milinda's Questions"), translated by T.W. Rhys-Davids as *The Questions of King Milinda*, Sacred Books of the East, vols. 35, 36 (Oxford: Clarendon Press, 1890, 1894); and *Visuddhimagga* ("The Path of Purification"), translated by Bhikkhu Nanamoli as *The Path of Purification* (Colombo: A. Semage, 1964).

Selected Mahayana Texts:

The Prajna-paramita sutras ("Perfection of Wisdom Discourses")

There are more than a dozen of these texts, varying in length from 100,000 lines to fourteen lines. The two of these which have had the greatest impact on Mahayana life and thought are *Prajna-paramita Hridaya Sutra* ("The Sutra on the Heart of the Perfection of Wisdom") and *Vajracchedika Prajnaparamita Sutra* ("The Sutra of the Diamond-cutting Perfection of Wisdom"), translated by Edward Conze in *Buddhist Wisdom Books* (London: Allen and Unwin, 1958).

Sad-dharma-pundarika Sutra ("The Sutra of the Lotus of the True Dharma")

Translated by H. Kern as *Saddharma-Pundarika or The Lotus of the True Law*, The Sacred Books of the East, vol. 21 (Oxford: Clarendon Press, 1884).

Sukhavati-vyuha ("Vision of the Pure Land")

Translated by E. B. Cowell, F. Max Muller, and J. Takakusu, in *Buddhist Mahayana Texts*, The Sacred Books of the East, vol. 49 (Oxford: Clarendon Press, 1894).

For selections from the whole Mahayan literature, see Edward Conze, *Buddhist Texts Through the Ages* (New York: Harper & Row, 1954).

Selected Reading List

Bechert, Heinz, and Richard Gombrich, eds. *The World of Buddhism: Buddhist Monks and Nuns in Society and Culture*. New York: Facts On File, 1984.

Bharati, Agehananda. *The Tantric Tradition*. Garden City, N.Y.: Anchor Books, 1970.

Blofeld, John. *The Tantric Mysticism of Tibet: A Practical Guide*. New York: Dutton, 1970.

Ch'en, Kenneth K.S. *Buddhism in China*. Princeton, N.J.: Princeton University Press, 1964.

Conze, Edward, et al., eds. *Buddhist Texts Through the Ages*. New York: Harper & Row, 1954.

————. *Buddhist Thought in India*. Ann Arbor: University of Michigan Press, Ann Arbor Paperbacks, 1967.

Cowell, E.B., F. Max Muller, and J. Takakusu, trans. *Buddhist Mahayana Texts. The Sacred Books of the East*, vol. 49. Edited by F. Max Muller). Oxford: Clarendon Press, 1894.

De Bary, William Theodore, ed. *The Buddhist Tradition*. New York: Modern Library, 1969.

Dumoulin, Heinrich. *A History of Zen Buddhism*. Translated by Paul Peachey. New York: Pantheon, 1963.

————, ed. *Buddhism in the Modern World*. New York: Macmillan, 1976.

Dutt, Sukumar. *Buddhist Monks and Monasteries of India*. London: Allen & Unwin, 1962.

Foucher, Alfred. *The Life of the Buddha According to the Ancient Texts and Monuments of India*. Abridged translation by Simone Brangier Boas. Middletown, Conn.: Wesleyan University Press, 1963.

Govinda, Anagarika Brahmacari. *The Psychological Attitude of Early Buddhist Philosophy*. London: Rider, 1961.

Kapleau, Philip. *The Three Pillars of Zen*. Boston: Beacon Press, 1968.

Kern, H., trans. *Saddharma-Pundarika or The Lotus of the True Law. The Sacred Books of the East*, vol. 21. Oxford: Clarendon Press, 1884.

Lamotte, Etienne. *Histoire du Bouddhisme indien des origines a l'ere Saka.* Reprint. Louvain: Publications Universitaires, 1967.

Lester, Robert C. *Theravada Buddhism in Southeast Asia.* Ann Arbor: University of Michigan Press, 1973.

Ling, Trevor O. *A Dictionary of Buddhism.* New York: Scribner, 1972.

Morgan, Kenneth William, ed. *The Path of the Buddha: Buddhism Interpreted by Buddhists.* New York: Ronald Press, 1956.

Murti, T.R.V. *The Central Philosophy of Buddhism.* London: Allen & Unwin, 1955.

Nanamoli, Thera, trans. *The Path of Purification (Visuddhimagga).* Colombo: Semage, 1956.

Nanaponika, Thera. *The Heart of Buddhist Meditation.* New York: Weiser, 1971.

Prebish, Charles S., ed. *Buddhism: A Modern Perspective.* University Park: Pennsylvania State University Press, 1975.

Rahula, Walpola. *What the Buddha Taught.* New York: Grove Press, 1974.

Reynolds, Frank E. *Guide to Buddhist Religion* (Bibliography). Boston: Hall, 1981.

Rhys Davids, T. W., trans. *Buddhist Suttas. The Sacred Books of the East,* vol. 11. Oxford: Clarendon Press, 1881.

————. *The Questions of King Milinda. The Sacred Books of the East,* vols. 35, 36. Oxford: Clarendon Press, 1890, 1894.

Sangharakshita, Bhikshu. *A Survey of Buddhism.* Bangalore: Indian Institute of World Culture, 1966.

Smith, Bardwell L., ed. *Unsui: A Diary of Zen Monastic Life.* Honolulu: University Press of Hawaii, East-West Center, 1973.

Suzuki, Diasetz Teitaro. *Introduction to Zen Buddhism.* New York: Grove Press, 1964.

————. *The Training of the Zen Buddhist Monk.* New York: University Books, 1965.

Suzuki, Shunryu. *Zen Mind, Beginner's Mind.* Tokyo: John Weatherhill, 1973.

Tambiah, S. J. *Buddhism and the Spirit Cults in North-east Thailand.* Cambridge: Cambridge University Press, 1970.

Thomas, Edward J. *The History of Buddhist Thought*. London: Routledge & Kegan Paul, 1963.

————. *The Life of Buddha as Legend and History*. London: Routledge & Kegan Paul, 1949.

Warren, Henry Clarke, trans. *Buddhism in Translations*. New York: Atheneum, 1984.

Wright, Arthur F. *Buddhism in Chinese History*. Stanford, Calif.: Stanford University Press, 1959.